YOURS, MINE &
WE DECIDED NOT TO HAVE
OURS

Cecelia Garceau

WinePress Publishing
MUKILTEO, WA 98275

Dedication

This book is dedicated to my loving husband, who loved each one of these children in a special way. Even when I couldn't stand mine the way they acted.

It is also dedicated to our seven precious children who, in spite of it all, we love, and only want their happiness. I hope they can forgive all the blunders and mistakes we have made in our lives.

All their names have been changed to protect the innocent.

Cover description

"Frank always said: 'Our family has to be like ducks on the pond for everything to be in God's order. The mom and dad duck out in front, and all the little ducks following behind. This is God's order, according to Scripture.'" _Ephesians 5:22-6:4 (Paraphrased)_

"...the husband is the head of the wife, as Christ is the Head of the church, His body, of which He is the Savior." _Ephesians 5:23 NIV (Holman, 1980)_

"...a man shall leave his father and mother and be united to his wife and the two shall become one flesh." _Ephesians 5:31 NIV (Holman, 1980)_

"In other words, in any family relationship, it should be husband, wife and then child or children..." Cecilia Garceau, Author

CONTENTS

INTRODUCTION TO MY LIFE

At the beginning of this chapter in my life, I was alone on a twenty-acre farm, raising three children, remodeling my old farmhouse, and working at a local insurance office in town. I was trying to put my life back together, alone and determined to make a go of it by myself. I was full of guilt for not being able to make my marriage of 16 years work. I hadn't believed in divorce and almost lost my health before I realized I had to get out of this relationship and save my children's life, what was left of my son's self-esteem, and maybe save his life, too—which at this point was almost beyond repair.

I didn't care if I had a man in my life ever again, but I had carefully made a list of what I wanted in a man if ever again I would care to meet someone. My list was very specific, so I knew that if I ever dated anyone, he would have to have most of the things on my list before I would go out with him on a second date. If I did go out with him again, I would test him as we dated to be sure he had the remaining things on my list before I got emotionally involved with him at any serious level. I knew it was too easy to fall in love with the wrong person. I have seen lots of people that fall in love with the wrong person and the same personality over and over, lead miserable lives, keep getting hurt, and wonder why. I did not want to get involved with someone and be miserable the rest of my life. I would rather be alone.

I knew I had to be very selective and I advise anyone alone in my position to do the same. I also had my children to consider. They needed a good man in their lives that was kind and would love them. That was a high priority, since they had already suffered enough in their short lives. He also had to be a Christian and have the same values I had.

I had talked to the children at great length and promised them I would be there for them; and they would have to learn to trust me no matter what I did. I assured them I would do what was best for them. They were too young to know what they needed in their lives. I see so many kids of divorced parents making decisions for their parents and running the parent's life. Remember, the children have no experience and the parents let them ruin one relationship after another. Most of the time their feelings are involved and mixed up with jealously and other selfish feelings. Sometimes they feel threatened in other ways and can't stand to think of their parent involved with anyone. Then a few years later, the children go on with their lives and the parent ends up left alone with no companion in their later years. The parents end up leading a very lonely life, only to realize that the children were making the decisions for them, when they shouldn't have let them.

You have to assure your children you love them. Make them realize that you are the adult and you will make the decisions for your life, not them. Never let it get started in the beginning. I also feel it is a good idea for you to be really sure about someone before you bring that person into their lives, let them get attached or let them feel that person is a part of their life.

Please remember to make a list of what you want in a mate. Stick to it no matter what your instincts tell you. Remember, you can't change someone much. Their basic personality will always be the same. If you really think about it, you really do know what you want; but be very specific and take lots of time and thought preparing your list. It is very important and it can change the course of your whole life.

2

FRANK'S LIFE

His life had really had its ups and downs. He had been divorced from his wife for quite awhile and was raising his two older children by himself. He was involved in building a new home, and was very ambitious. He had many friends that were always telling him how to run his life and what was best for him. I know their intentions were good, but they don't always know what's best for you. He had many insecurities in his life from previous disappointments with women. He was so insecure about everything he did. Every time he would do something, he would ask me, "Is there anything you want me to change and am I doing everything right?"

This was very hard, but I soon realized after our relationship started that the scars he had were deep, like mine, and would surface every so often in our relationship. One day after we had been dating for sometime, I was in a store I found this little plaque with a mirror on it. It said: *I love you just the way you are.* Every time he questioned his abilities to please me, I would make him look into this mirror and repeat the saying, "I love you just the way you are." He needed to rebuild his self-confidence, and he needed reassurance that God loved him the way he was, unconditionally. He loves us just the way we are, so you should always love yourself and anyone else the way they are.

We had lots of long talks about this, but we both knew it would only take time to heal our deep wounds. He was at a point that he didn't have much self-confidence left and didn't know what he could be to a woman, and was scared of any more relationships. He had made his church, friends and kids his whole life. His friends tried to help him in every way they could, but they could not fill the empty hole he had in his heart and life that only a woman could fill.

He was always taking people in and helping them. He was a very giving man. He would help them get their mental and spiritual lives straightened out. He would spend a lot of time praying with them and for them, and tried to help them in every way he could. Just before I met him, he had taken in a young man who was really mixed up about life. He had found him along the road one day hitchhiking and had picked him up and took him home. He was helping him get his life going again. He lived with Frank for a while and they became very good friends. Later, he went on and was able to get his life going again and lead a successful life. Frank had dreams and aspirations of how a relationship should be, but felt this may never happen to him in his lifetime. He began to wonder if he had unrealistic ideas of what he could have in a wife and a relationship. That didn't stop him from dreaming, hoping someday he would have a wife and a friend to share his life with just like he had dreamed of.

3

CAUGHT BY THE MONGOOSE

You see this all began with a mongoose. If you don't know what a mongoose is, the definition is:

Furry mammal, that is roughly eighteen inches long, and they have a pointed head, small ears, slender body, generally dark coat, a long bushy tapering tail, short legs and four or five toes, and nonretractable claws on each leg. Some are weasel-like while others are more dog-like. They seem to be very agile and run in leaps, they are a very fast animal and can kill a cobra by smartly stepping aside when the snake strikes and pouncing on the snakes head from above. They crack the snake's skull with one bite.

So you see they are a very vicious animal. They usually sleep during the day and are out preying on their victims at night.

I had worked for a gentleman who had a great sense of humor. He had built this mongoose cage with an old, net enclosure out front, where the mongoose could come out and be seen. But, when it was sleeping, you could only see his mangy tail sticking out into the screened enclosure. What made it look more vicious were the bones lying about in the screened enclosure and you could see the mongoose's tail curled up in the enclosure. Of course, you would explain that these bones were from previous victims he had ate. Every time the gentleman I worked for would hire a new girl in the office, he would pull this mongoose story on them. You could always tell because you could hear them scream from the back room clear up in the front office. You knew that someone new had been initiated into the fold when he let the mongoose's fury loose on them for the first time.

There was a lid on the top of the cage that could be slid open, so you could take your chances and have a first-hand view of this mean, vicious creature. As you slid the top of the cage open, this stuffed animal was on a spring and would come flying out to greet you, in a not so interesting fashion, to give you a real look at what was inside. Startling the most unsuspecting person to scream and run from this creature they had heard so much about.

I had been working for this insurance agency for awhile, when one day I decided to borrow this cage from my previous employer and show my fellow employees its wrath and bring some interesting activity to the office. So I picked up the mongoose that morning from my previous employer and brought it into our office for a day. I showed it to my employers. They thought this would be great fun and began to show people themselves. We had so much fun all day telling people the detailed, blow by blow story about this terrible mongoose and how vicious he was. Of course, when you got them real interested, then you

14

would get them huddled over top of the cage to take a peak and pull the lid off the top of the cage, slowly, as not to disturb this animal, and really give them a closer look. This furry stuffed animal would come flying out at them, sometimes flying clear across the room, other times just straight up in the air in front of them. Of course, the stories you had told them about this animal before you released this creature didn't help with the startling appearance of this stuffed animal flying out at them.

Well, it just so happened this particular afternoon, there was a certain plumber looking for business insurance to start up his new plumbing business. He came into the office where I worked for an insurance quote to get his business started. I was very busy, and rather behind because of all the distractions I had that day from our mongoose fun. I looked up as the door opened and this sparky guy walked in, and you could see he was a very curious person. Guess what was the first thing that caught his eye as he stepped up to the counter. Right, the mongoose cage sitting behind the counter, big as life, waiting for its next victim to ask, "What is that?" That was exactly what he asked. I didn't want to show him, ha, but I thought for a minute and decided I didn't want to disappoint him. I began my tale once again.

I began telling him about this dangerous mongoose. I told him about how he slept during the day and was nocturnal, but was very vicious if awoke during its resting time. Of course, we really had the story down pat by now. I told him about his big teeth and pointed out the bones in the screened-in enclosure on the front of the cage, where you could see his mangy tail sticking out. I told him the whole blow by blow story and when I finished, I explained to him that if he leaned over the top of the cage, I would pull the door open slowly so he could get a quick, first-hand look at this creature. I told him to be very quiet and careful not to wake him up and make him mad. Being the curious person he was, even though he was suspicious about the story and this cage, he leaned over the top of the cage carefully. I slowly slid the lid open so he could see the mongoose. Of course, I slid it just enough to engage the mongoose's furry upon him. On its mission of mercy, or something like that, it came flying out at him. Well, he jumped, hollered and ran, all at the same time, ending up on top of a nearby chair.

You see, I really got his attention right away. I know to this day, he has not forgotten this experience, but it hasn't changed his curious nature. He still has to explore the unknown. I always said, after living with a Frenchman for a few years, I understood why the French were explorers, because they are always so curious about everything that is going on and want to know how and why it works.

After the initial shock of all this excitement was over, we got down to business and he got his insurance quote and left. Of course, the girls in the office were always matchmaking and they were busy checking out his file and informing me he was single, and suggested I look into this man.

I was not interested in a relationship of any kind. I had been hurt and was very afraid of getting involved with anyone. I was not sure I would see him again. We all went on with our work and finished the day, still laughing about our day with the mongoose's fury. I don't think any of us got much work done, we were having so much fun that day at everyone else expense. It seemed like every time I got started with my work, someone would come through the door and my boss would say, "Show them our visitor....." Of course then everyone in the office would get involved, so they could be there for the excitement when it was released from its resting place, once again.

4

DIVINE APPOINTMENT

Much to my surprise, the Lord had something else planned for us. On the following weekend, I had a yard sale with a girlfriend and guess who showed up at the yard sale. You know already. He was looking for a helmet for his son, who had just gotten a small motorcycle. We had a good visit while he was looking around at what we had for sale. While we were talking I remembered he was a plumber. I decided I would ask him some questions about the trouble I was having with my irrigation pump on my farm. I was sure he would have some solutions to solve the problem I was having with my pump. As we were talking I explained to him that I had a twenty-acre farm, and was in the middle of remodeling my home. I really had a big load to handle with my farm, job and three children to support and take care of . The financial load and the emotional load was a lot for a single mom.

After I had finished telling him about the trouble I was having with my pump, of course he was still curious, and said, "Why doesn't your husband take care of the pump or doesn't he understand how to do it?" I informed him I wasn't married anymore and I was capable of taking care of it myself, but at times there were things I needed help with, but most of the time my son, who was 13, and I managed pretty well.

He told me later, "Boy was I excited when I heard that you were not married, bells and whistles went off…" But he played it cool at the time and went on talking. He told me later that he was always seeing women that he admired, but finding out later that they were married, and it lead to another disappointment. He told me he was much too nervous to make a move or get involved at that point. He had to make his plan. But he did say before he left, "If you don't get your pump going, let me know, I will come by and help you figure it out."

With the entire weekend to ponder all of this, he must have made a decision to contact me again. On Monday, after I had already made plans for lunch, at 11:59 the telephone rang at my office. It was for me, a call from guess who, wanting to know if I could go to lunch that day. Of course he didn't wait until the last minute or anything. He told me later that he had started dialing at 11:00. He would start to dial and chicken out and hang up before he finished dialing my number. He did this repeatedly for an hour before being able to dial that final number and make the connection to my work number. Of course by that time, I usually already had made my lunch plans. I felt bad and said, "Call me again sometime and we will go to lunch." I guess once he had made the call, it got easier because the next day at 11:00 he called and invited me to go to lunch.

Lunch time came and he picked me up at my office at 12:00 right on schedule, and we had a great lunch. We found we had lots in common. He loved the farm, coming from a farm background, and of course there was my pump that I still needed help with. He asked me if I had tried the suggestions he had given me and if I had any success at solving the problem with the pump. I told him I didn't have much success so he suggested that he come over on Sunday and take a look at it to be able to see what he could do to help. Our time seemed to go so fast, and lunch was soon over. As we headed back to the office, I thought, *Well if he is nice enough to take his Sunday afternoon to help me the least I could do is invite him and his kids out for dinner.* So I extended the invitation for dinner on Sunday when we could work on the pump and he could see my farm. As I sat back down at my desk, I wondered how this happened. Was this a date? No. Oh well, it was the least I could do. I would get my pump fixed and we would have a good visit, no harm in that. I had seen some very caring qualities in him and several other things I had on my list, if I was looking, which I assured myself I was not.

Sunday came and we were together again, this time with five children, ages 14,13,12,11,5. I was a bit nervous, but he came and we had a nice dinner and later spent a lot of time walking around my farm and talking about our lives. Then there was the pump. He checked it over and was able to fix the problem.

What a big relief for me because the weather was still hot, and the pump had to run correctly to irrigate the pasture so the cattle would have plenty of feed. I had bought the calves in the spring and planned on selling them in the fall. The income helped to make my payment on my home and farm. So it was pretty important not to let the grass dry up and the feed be all gone.

I was grateful, and the kids had a real good time. He loved the dinner I fixed, of course it was meat, potatoes and gravy. Since he was raised on a farm in North Dakota, a meal was not a meal without these staples. This was a big part of his upbringing, a good meal, and I really made an impression on his heart, of course his stomach too. I did not realize it, I always cooked that way. They say the way to a man's heart is through his stomach, and with this particular man, that was very true.

Well we said our good-byes, and he left with his family. Our two older daughters really had a good time. They rode horses and talked a lot, they were close to the same age and had a lot in common to share and talk about. Well, at least everything went well. We all had a great day together and a wonderful time enjoying each other's company and the farm and all it had to offer. And, of course, I got my pump fixed. The girls left promising they would call each other soon, we said good-bye, not sure when our paths would ever cross again.

5

THE PLOT THICKENS

He called me several times for lunch after that and we always enjoyed our time together. The girls managed to get us together for some outings, and in fact the kids began plotting on how to get us all together for more than we were ready for. On several occasions, they called each other and made plans to see each other. Of course, it usually involved us one way or another when the kids got together, since they did not drive yet. As time went on, our family outings became more frequent and our kids had great times together. They all wanted a family atmosphere and loved doing family things.

One particular outing, we all went to the annual county fair. We all had a great day and the kids enjoyed the excitement of it all. The only problem was we met lots of our friends there, and of course everyone wanted to know how long we had been seeing each other and all the details. We were not ready for that. We were only entertaining our families and we did not give anyone much information regarding the subject. I was really reserved about our relationship and did not like showing any affection towards him. In fact, he shared with me later that the first time he kissed me, after the fair that day, it was the coldest kiss he ever had. But something made him press on with our relationship and our times together continued. Most of the time we would try and control any feelings we might have and it would make a strain on our times together.

One evening the kids planned for us to have supper together at the farm. We were sitting on the couch after supper, and suddenly the lights went dim and soft music started playing. That was really embarrassing. Neither of us were ready for that, but the kids continued matchmaking and plotting our course. You see that had to be from God, because to have 5 kids and have them all happy about our times together and our relationship, was a miracle in itself. We continued having fun, picnics and many neat outings and lots of good times on the farm together. We all loved the farm. These were indeed memorable experiences for all of us.

I watched this man very carefully, to see if he had other things on my list. I was always testing him to see if he would meet more requirements on "the list." Each time we dated, I found out more and more about him. I was still determined that I was not going to fall in love with the wrong person, and was determined to stick to my list. As I watched this man from the very beginning of our relationship, he had so many of the qualities I had on my list, that I was getting worried. Maybe I should continue to see him and put him through more tests to see if he could pass. He would surely fail, and I would be safe from even considering going on with this relationship.

One outing I remember in particular, we had gone out target practicing. When we went to get back into the car to leave to go home, he helped me in my side of the car, and went over to get into his side. Of course his daughter jumped in when he opened the car door, and slid in between us. I was startled, but didn't say anything. He promptly got out of the car and moved me over next to him and explained to his daughter that she needed to sit by the door on the other side, and not in between us.

Oh no, he passed another test.

I knew at that point, I was special to him and that I was going to be first in his life. You see, that really made me understand something about my requirements that a couple must be first in each other's life to have a good relationship. I know that this was hard on his daughter, but children have to be made to understand at times that men and women need a special relationship and closeness apart from the children. Had this not happened this way, it could have changed the course of our relationship.

It was fall and hunting season was drawing near, my son had always wanted to go hunting. Frank loved to hunt and had done lots of hunting as a boy in North Dakota. They talked at great lengths about his hunting experiences as a boy. They began to get all excited about taking a hunting trip, and of course a hunting trip was eventually planned. This was the highlight of my son's life, a dream come true for him. After the trip was planned, we decided that his son, who was more of a bookworm and wasn't too interested in hunting, needed to go too.

We knew it would be good for both boys to share this time together. They spent many hours talking and making their plans for the trip.

6

DEAR SEASON

Well the day finally came. They loaded up food, rifles, and tons of supplies and off they went to the woods for the hunt. They hunted hard for three days, and finally Dale spotted a small buck. He aimed, shot and killed his first deer. What an exciting time for a young boy. They had a wonderful trip and even with only getting one deer it was still memorable, and of course the stories got bigger and bigger by the time they reached home. Dale had a great time and was beginning to care a great deal about this man who had come into his life. After all the abuse he had from his father, it was hard for him to let anyone get close to him. He had very low self-esteem and was afraid to trust anyone. I noticed that when anyone tried to get close to him, he would suddenly turn on them and try to destroy the relationship and love they felt for him. I guess he did not feel worthy of love. It was hard to understand what was going on in his mind. He had been hurt so bad, and trusted no one with his feelings and especially didn't want anyone close enough for a relationship with him.

A few weeks later, he was alone with Frank, He looked up at him and said, "When are you going to tell my mother the question?" Frank did not know how to answer this complex question at this time. Of course, Dale meant, "When are you going to ask my mother to marry you?"

It also meant, *I approve of you. I want you for my father*, although he could not tell him that at the time. The kids were ready to move on with this relationship, but we weren't ready at all.

At this time, I was also in the middle of remodeling this old farmhouse I was living in. I had tore out all the old, wide baseboards and the old wall board. I was doing my own version of remodeling, what little I knew. I hadn't done anything like this before, but I was determined to turn this old house into something nice, in spite of its pitfalls.

As Frank came over I began to explain my projects to him and he began to help me. He knew quite a lot about construction and he had just finished building a new home in a nearby town just before we met, so he had a lot of knowledge in building and he had been around lots of construction projects during his career as a plumber. I figured this would be an excellent time to see if he could pass the "temper test" on my list because I knew how construction projects test your patience and tolerance levels.

You see, in my first marriage, I was used to starting a project and seeing terrible temper flare-ups. Things would fly and words would become very upsetting and I would be sick to my stomach by the time the project was underway. So I was really hesitant to get involved in this test, but I knew I had to try for my list's sake. It took me years to get over getting sick when we would start a project. I had a lot of old scars that were opened up for a long time. Even after I trusted Frank, it took a long time to get over those reactions that I had had for so long. So the day came and I hung a tool belt on him and put 5 kids underfoot and watched him very carefully doing my projects and still keeping his cool. Indeed, this project would be the ultimate test if he could pass it. I watched each time he would set his hammer down. My youngest daughter, Cindy would pick up his hammer and begin pounding with it and she would nail all the boards he was using for the project together before he got back to his hammer. When he would go to reach for them, they were all nailed and she was off with his hammer. He would patiently retrieve his hammer, go on and take out the nails she had put in his boards, time after time. I could see he had patience with a capital P. I had never seen this in any man. As this project continued. I became very found of him, but I was still scared and so was he of showing our feelings to each other. We still were not able to admit to each other that we might care for each other in a special way.

One afternoon as we were working on the house, I came out for a few minutes on the front porch for some air. I stood there for a few minutes hearing a familiar sound, but not quite able to identify what it was. As I listened, I began to realize it was my son's voice. He was yelling for help from a distance and it sounded like it was coming from down on the ditch-bank road behind the barn. I knew he had been walking the ditch road and hunting earlier that day which he did so often, which meant he was carrying his gun with him. I had all these visions and I began running as fast as I could down to the ditch road, where I followed his screams to where he was.

As I came close, I could see him lying on the ground where he had fallen and he was holding his leg near the hip and screaming with pain. I didn't know what to do, but I knew I had to get him some help so I ran back to the house screaming for Frank. He came running out of the house and we both jumped in the car and we drove down the ditch-bank road where my son lay. We jumped out of the car and began examining him for gunshot wounds, but there weren't any, that was a relief, but we still didn't know what was wrong. It appeared that something had happened to his hip or upper leg. So we loaded him in the car screaming with pain, and began heading for the hospital. We finally arrived and got him out of the car, and into the x-ray room so they could determine what had happened to him.

In a little while, the doctor came out and told me he had checked the x-rays and discovered that my son had knocked the ball out of his hip socket. He would have to be taken to a specialist about thirty miles away by ambulance to have the operation that would correct this injury. He explained to us that in the future with injuries, you should never move anyone hurt especially load them into a car, because you could really cause them some damage. We hadn't even thought of that we just wanted to get him some help. We never thought that just falling could do so much damage that would be so serious.

They loaded him in the ambulance and were off to a hospital thirty miles away, and we followed in the car and arrived at the hospital shortly after he did. They got him settled and were scheduling him for surgery early the next morning to put pins through the leg and through the hip socket to hold it all together once again so it could heal in place. I was very upset, but I knew I had to get home and get some rest so I could be there for him before surgery the next morning. Frank looked at me and we decided that we needed to leave since Dale was finally resting with the help of medication. So we headed home to get some rest for the big day we had in store tomorrow,.

Frank was very quiet all the way home, I knew there was something on his mind that he could not talk about to me at this time. I could see how much he cared for this boy, but I knew there was something about this quietness, much deeper than I could visualize. After we had driven a few more miles I could see he wanted to talk, but I could see it was not easy for him to start. He finally said he had to get this out and talk about it with me.

We had never talked about personal things or our close feelings before so this was a new experience. He told me that he could not go to the hospital with me in the morning. He too had scars that were so deep and so open he could not face another hospital encounter in his life. There had been a heartbreaking hospital scene in his past with his first wife that had left him devastated and unable to face another hospital scene that might be comparable. He realized that this scene would be a reminder of what he had gone through in the past. He was worried that Dale's father would show up and make a scene because Frank was by his side. He could not bear to be reminded of this situation. He had tried to block all this out for many years and this would bring flashbacks of so many hurts.

As we talked I understood why he had told me he could not go with me to the hospital. I understood his pain and told him that it was OK if he didn't come with me, although I really would have liked him to be there with me and I knew Dale needed him there badly. He loved him so much and needed his support, but I did not want to bring any more pain into his life to deal with. I could see the anguish on his face from just telling me

about it. I don't know if he had talked about this to anyone since all this had happened and it had opened up
some old deep wounds.

He dropped me off at my house and I assured him I
would be OK and that I didn't want to bring him any more
pain. We were both drained emotionally and I went in the
house and went to bed and tried to get some sleep for the
next day's ordeal. I awoke early. I didn't get much sleep
and I knew I had to drive thirty miles to the hospital and
I wanted to be there before Dale went into surgery. I was
busy getting ready to leave when the telephone rang.

It was Frank.

I was so tickled to hear his voice, I needed some moral
support about that time. He said, after a pause, "I am
going with you to the hospital this morning. I care about
you and Dale too much to let you go through this by
yourself." That was really refreshing to me, and I began
doing some deep thinking about this unselfish man.

Soon he was there to pick me up, and we were off to the
hospital. On the way he was very quiet. I knew he was worrying about what was going to take place that day, and praying that he would not have to encounter any pain and have
all those old hurts surface. We both knew, but we never
spoke about this. We just both knew it was on our minds.

I prayed that Dale would be OK, and that Frank
would not have to face anything terrible because of his
unselfishness. I told him how much his coming with me
meant to me, and I didn't realize it, but it was the first
time I was able to express myself to him. I was so grateful
for his company and support during those hours I had to
wait for my son to come out of surgery, and I knew what
it would mean to Dale when he came out of surgery and
see Frank standing there at his side.

7

THE TURNING POINT

Just before Dale headed into surgery, he was pleading with me not to let his dad know he was in the hospital. I had called his grandparents the night before when I had gotten home from the hospital and told them about the accident. We were very close, and they were wonderful people and cared very much for their grandchildren. I was not aware that they had called their son and told him what had happened, and had told him that he needed to be there to see his son. Dale was very bitter against his father, and after all the hard years it seemed very sad for me.

I promised Dale I would not call his father so he would settle down before he headed in for surgery, and be in a good frame of mind while he was going through all this pain. We waited a long time before the doctor came out and brought the x-rays and showed us the large pins they had used to pin the hip socket back into place. They had pinned from one side of his leg to the other.

Soon, we were notified that he was in recovery and we headed up to Dale's room to be there when he came out of the anesthesia and was beginning to wake up. The minute Dale arrived in the room, still rather out of it from surgery, he began calling for Frank to be by his side, and he did not want anyone else there. He seemed to feel great comfort by having this man at his side, and he did not care if anyone else was in the room. Dale felt great love for this man, and he knew that Frank loved him and it was a love and a kindness he had never experienced before in his life.

Suddenly, as he began to focus on what was going on I heard a noise and looked up and there was his father coming through the door. I began to get very tense, and as soon as Dale saw him, he began yelling that he did not want his father there and for him to leave. He only wanted Frank there by his side and he made it very clear to everyone, even in the state he was in. Frank tried to console him and explain to him that his dad wanted to see him, but to no avail. He just kept calling for Frank to stay by his side. It was very uncomfortable for everyone. I could see the strain on Frank's face, and suddenly he said he needed to leave for awhile because he could not bear this encounter and could not see any way to solve it except to leave for awhile. So he explained to Dale that he had to leave for a short while and he would be back soon.

As he left, Dale's grandparents appeared and Dale seemed to settle down a little more, but would not look or speak to his father. As he faded in and out he kept calling for Frank to come back and I could see he was still very upset with me because his father had showed up. I tried to explain to him that I had not called him and shortly his grandparents spoke up and told him they had made the call. I had hoped all this had not been too much for Frank, but I did not know what to do to ease this upsetting time for everyone. Soon Dale's dad left, what a relief, and a short time later Frank appeared at the door. I was so glad to see him and so was Dale, it even brought a smile to his face. It had been a very hard day and it was soon evening and we decided to go home and check on the other children and let Dale get some rest and get some ourselves. As we headed home, I was so thankful that we had all survived this ordeal, it was a tough one for everyone involved.

One evening after I had gotten home from the hospital and was sitting relaxing at home after dinner, there was a knock on the door. When I looked out there was Frank standing at my door. I opened it surprised to see him, he explained to me that he had been at a Christian men's' business meeting and in the middle of the meeting, after battling his feelings for some time that he wanted to come see me, he could not stand it any longer and he left the meeting and headed for my house and there he was at my door.

Frank had been pretty reserved up to this point about coming over by himself. We both had a lot of reservations about getting too close, but this had been a growing time for us while my son was hurt and we both had a lot of time to think about things throughout this time we had spent caring for my son in the hospital. It didn't help our fears about caring about one another, but something had changed. There he stood as he explained why he was at my door and why he had left his meeting. He came in and we sat and shared a lot that evening that we had never shared before.

In the weeks to follow as I was driving back and forth from the hospital, I also had a lot of time to think and do some soul searching. When I would get home, Frank would be there at my house to greet me and was working on my remodeling projects whenever he had time. I was still in the middle of this mess and had really gotten behind with my son in the hospital. I could not believe the changes that were taking place in this old house because of this kind man's help.

Towards the end of my son's stay in the hospital as I was driving home one evening, thinking as I was driving, I suddenly came to a realization. I really did care a lot about this man. He had everything on "the list." Why was I dragging my feet so hard, what was I waiting for?

I decided right then and there that I had to tell him how I felt even at the risk of losing him. I knew he was afraid, too, and it might scare him away. As soon as I got home, I called him and asked him to come over that evening. After I called him, my stomach was in real turmoil. Had I made the right decision to do this?

When he came over it was even harder. I had to work up the courage some how and get this over with. After a short while we sat down and began talking and I worked up the courage to tell him how I felt about him, and our relationship. He looked very startled at first, but I could see a softness come over him and then he began to speak. I could tell this was hard for him too, but he began to speak. I cringed, what was he going to say? He told me that he had wanted to tell me how he felt about me for quite some time, but he too was afraid of losing me when he opened up, it was a wonderful evening as our love was growing to a much deeper dimension.

This was indeed a turning point in our relationship and after this we began to grow closer and closer with each day . It was also a scary time, hoping we had made the right decision for our lives to open up to each other, and wondering if we were really ready for all this.

My son finally got home from the hospital, and we tried to resume a halfway-normal life with him on crutches, if that is possible. It was very hard, he was not the sitting, patient type. He was always very active outside and with him having to sit it was hard on all of us. Time seemed to march on and we spent more and more enjoyable time together as a family and in private. Frank was there every evening and on weekends we spent every moment we could together, neither of us had ever experienced what we were experiencing in our relationship. We could not get enough of what was happening in our lives together.

Christmas was drawing near and the weather had begun to turn cold. Frank came over and made sure we had enough wood for our woodstove, and we went on several trips to get firewood in the nearby hills. Our family was growing very close, and so were we with each passing day.

We had a wonderful Christmas together that was the most wonderful peaceful Christmas we had ever experienced. We were all sitting around in the evening after supper and my youngest daughter Cindy was sitting on Frank's lap sucking her thumb and stroking his fine hair, as she loved to do. She looked up at Frank and said, "I love you." He was her security blanket and he loved her like his own. It was a painful time because we wanted to be together and did a lot of serious talking in the evenings when he would come over.

8

WEDDING BELLS

One Friday evening in January, Frank came over and we were having a very serious talk about each other and our feelings. We talked about being together what was so important to both of us and we even talked about just living together. But we knew that was not right and we had to care enough about each other to trust each other to build a life together. It seems like the easy way out, but it isn't and we knew the impact that living together would make on our children and we knew deep down that was not the kind of example we wanted to show our children for there lives.

Parents: Please always remember your responsibility to be an example to your children and to God's commandments. I heard a saying one time:

Home....where life makes up its mind.

You can't teach your children what you don't possess yourself. Please keep this in mind, and think very carefully about the choices you make and the impact on your family.

We finally came to the decision that we cared enough about each other to build a life together and make a commitment to get married. We spent many hours talking that evening and it was getting late and the kids were getting tired. We decided it was time to set a date to get married and we knew we were weary of being apart, and when we were apart wanting to be together.

We looked at each other and almost said simultaneously, "Well, why don't we just go and get married as soon as possible? Why wait? Let's tell the children?

So we gathered all the children in the living room, and told them the news. They were jumping up and down and running about so excited and were so anxious to tell all their friends.

After we had settled them down somewhat, we began talking about tomorrow when everyone would know our plans, because we knew the kids would not keep quiet about this. Even our friends and family would know and we wanted to keep everyone out of our business and our plans. We just wanted it to be the two of us and no friendly advice from loved ones and well-meaning friends.

We had worked so hard to this point of keeping everyone else out of our relationship and not letting them influence our decisions about one another. This was a rather sore spot with his friends in particular for quite awhile after we got married, because they were not included in our plans, and they were used to being involved in his life. So as we kept talking, it became clear to us we had to do what we were going to do right then and there and not wait to set a date. So we made a decision to leave for Coeur d' Alene, Idaho, the next morning, where there was no waiting period to get married and it would just involve the two of us.

The next morning was eventful. The first thing, Frank got a call from a friend who owned a dairy and they had been close friends for a long time He was having difficulty with his plumbing at the dairy, so he called Frank early that morning to come help him fix his plumbing in his dairy so he could get his cows milked. I knew this was important, but on our wedding day?

Frank could not say no, so I went with him out to fix the plumbing and we giggled as we kept our secret and made a pact that we would leave as soon as we were finished with the plumbing repairs. The weather was beginning to deteriorate very fast, and it was snowing hard, but we were determined not to let anything or anyone interfere with our plan.

We had made our plan and we were so excited about our lives together, not even a snow storm could stand in our way at this point. By the time we left, it was snowing and blowing but we were in "la-la land," Off we went in the storm, ready to make our commitment to one another, and we knew if we did not take this opportunity, we might miss it and we would have to take time to plan all this over again to get away.

It was a five-hour drive, very slow in the blizzard, but we were happy and we knew we had made the right choice. We were so much in love. We stopped on the way and bought two gold bands. We were really ready now in every way.

We finally arrived and found out where the wedding chapel was and we excitedly drove up to the "Hitching Post" that was a famous marriage chapel, but as we got out of the car in front we noticed a big sign in the window, it said: CLOSED. We looked at each other and decided to look closer, and as we did, we discovered it was not open on Saturday or Sunday. This was Saturday. We had never thought of this...*now what*?

Well, we talked it over and decided that we had until Monday before we could get married and in all of our excitement we had not thought about things being closed on the weekends. Well, we decided that since we were already there and wanted to get married, maybe we should just stay until Monday. I guess we could have our honeymoon first, a little backwards, but it worked, and then get married on Monday when everything opened up. What choice did we have? Here we were. So we checked into a motel close by and enjoyed our weekend, and our honeymoon. We would show them. But I informed him on Monday I was not going home without being married. Monday came quickly and everyone was in the marrying business again, so we were off to the courthouse to get our license and go through all the procedures we had to go through to get married...*finally*. We were amazed there were a lot of couples there to get married on Monday morning. Some had driven all night from miles away. We met one special couple who ended up standing up for us when we got married and then we stood up for them as they exchanged their vows. They had also eloped and did not want their families to interfere with their lives. They were so cute, they were 83 and 75, and were very special people, and in love.

It was a special ceremony and we even had a nice minister there. One of our concerns was to have a Christian wedding and here was a wonderful Foursquare pastor to perform the ceremony, which meant a lot to both of us.

After we both were married, the four of us went out for lunch. Of course, everyone in the town was involved in these numerous weddings that take place in this small town. It was a big part of their economy and so they were prepared and had small wedding cakes baked for just this occasion and they brought each one of us a cake after our lunch. They really tried to make everyone's wedding special for them.

Unfortunately, tomorrow we had to face reality and head home and start our lives together and handle the everyday problems. But we would enjoy today and our wonderful day together and this very special time we had shared together.

The next morning, we loaded up the car and headed home excited about our lives, not really knowing what all we had in store for us with five children to face and five different personalities and each one with their own ideas.

We finally reached home and as we entered the house, we noticed our kids had everything decorated and they had planned a wedding party for us. It was so special and they had invited some neighbors and a few friends in. They had also made a card for us and had collected $3.00 for a wedding gift. It was so special and we realized they had done a lot of work planning this party. It was simple, but great and it really meant a lot to us.

After the party was over, Cindy crawled up in Frank's lap, as she usually did in the evening and looked him right in the eye, and said, "Does this mean you got to spend the night?"

We all laughed and assured her that he would be spending the night for a long time, and that was a normal procedure for married couples.

9

NEWLYWED BLISS

Well, married life began with a bang, not like most couples who start out with just the two of them. Five children makes things considerably different. It is hard enough for couples to learn about each other and struggle working things out. We had lots of real-life decisions to make about where to live and how to combine these two families and households, the best we knew how.

Frank had just built a new home in a neighboring town, which had lots of room and was very nice. The other choice we had was the old farmhouse I lived in, still in need of repair, but sitting on 20 acres. We only had three small bedrooms. There was a basement we looked over that and decided we could use that space, not fancy but an extra bedroom.

I did not feel comfortable about moving into his new home. It had been their home and that was their territory and I realized it would be hard to move in and feel it was my home and most of the control of that household had been given to his daughter. It didn't seem like it would be the best decision for us, we also knew that the farm would be the best place to raise the children, where they could have outside activities and chores and be away from town. This would give us more control on where they were and who they were with, because they could not go to town without a ride from us. We began making plans to sell his home and move to the farm.

It became very cozy when we started putting everyone in one house. Suddenly we discovered there was no place for us to hide, we couldn't find any privacy. If you can imagine newlyweds with ten eyes following you where ever you go and whatever you do. This was not an easy situation, but the time was not right to change anything, we would just make the best of it and keep going, and keep our privacy on hold.

As we settled in with all these different personalities, the fun really began. Something had changed with the children's attitudes, as we became an authority in their lives. Opposition began forming to everything we did and said, and of course Frank's children had been alone with him for along time and there was lots of mixed feelings flying at us everywhere. They seemed to fluctuate between jealousy and resentment most of the time. It was very confusing and we had to get a handle on all this before it became a problem between us. Frank and I enjoyed such a neat relationship together and were so happy just to be together.

As I look back, I am sure many times his children felt that I had taken their father away from them, because he had been the main parent in their lives and they had no interference in that relationship. I am sure they missed their dad's constant attention. He had just poured his time and life into them every day. They very seldom had any time with their mother and it made it harder for them to share their father, and I am sure they were scared of losing his love and attention. You understand these feelings, but it does not make it any easier to deal with the attitudes towards you.

I know to this day there is still some resentment and confusion in this area. I don't know if we will ever reach a peace about this. I pray as they develop their own relationships and families, they will see how important it is for couples to be close and that they can still love their children in a special way, but different than the love they feel for their spouse. You hope they will know there is always a special bond between parents and children and that there is room in everyone's life and heart to love both. It is a hard thing to understand and a harder thing to deal with. I don't know if the children even understand their own feelings.

My older son thought he was the man of the house and that he should run the farm the way he had been running things. It worked fine and why should this man come in and change things. Even though he loved Frank, there was resentment and conflict. The two older girls, well, what one didn't think of the other one did. Lisa and Debbie became very close which was very hard on my younger daughter, Cindy. She became very jealous of their relationship and being so much younger, she did not share much in common with them and their private conversations about boys, makeup, etc. She was not used to sharing her sister and most of the time they did not want her to be bothering them or snooping in their business, because if she overheard their plans, she would always tell on them and get them into trouble.

Dale and Matt were very opposite. Dale was a very outdoors person, very busy all the time, and Matt was a very quiet boy, very studious and sensitive, almost withdrawn from society. He spent his life with his nose in a book and did not care if he had any friends or any outside interests. Books were his retreat from everything, including facing life and its problems. His father always felt sorry for him because he did not have a mother's influence in his life. Having to leave his mother at a young age had taken its toll on his life and personality.

I remember Frank coming home those first few weeks, sitting Matt down and saying, "Now Matt, tell me all the things that happened to you today, and we will work through them." Of course Matt would start crying and going through all the bad things that had happened to him that day and all the bad things that were said to him, I listened several days and was appalled at what I heard. How could this young man find any happiness or survive this world dwelling only on the bad things in his life? I realized other kids usually picked on the studious kids and made fun of them, and Matt had to put up with a lot of this type of teasing. I felt my husband and I must have a heart to heart talk about this very soon and try and discuss this sensitive problem. I knew it would be hard because his instincts were so strong to protect this boy, many times even from me. I could not in good conscience let this go on and let him feel sorry for this boy who had so much going for him and a loving father and a good home, much more than most children. I knew somehow I had to convince him he had to dwell on the positive things in his life to find some peace with life.

We learned right away never to discuss a problem in front of the children, and we had made a pact to make our decisions and discuss any problems behind closed doors.

Then we would arrive at a decision together about the problem, and come out united in our decision, sometimes after much discussion. This is the only way you can do it and become united in your decision making and then no one else knows who was for the decision and who was against it.

During one of our behind-the-door discussions, I asked my husband, "Do you realize what you are doing to Matt's life in the name of love? I know you only mean well, but I am deeply concerned about this boy and feel that we have to work on dwelling on the positive side of his life. There is so much negative in everyone's life, that we need lots of positive input to keep going in life."

After much discussion, Frank was finally able to realize he needed to make an effort to change their discussions. I knew it would be very hard for him and draining to try and change their talks, but I felt it was so important, especially for his son, and for all of us that were involved in his life. I suggested that everyday when they had their talks, that Frank start out with, "Tell me what good things happened to you today," and only talk about the positive. I felt this would make his son see a whole new side of life that he had not been shown before, or hadn't thought about. This was very hard for his dad. He listened to me and did realize this was important, and that maybe things needed to change. After our talk, I could hear him trying each day to make a change in his son's life for the better when they would have their talks, but it was a difficult task for both.

You always have the feeling when you suggest something that is hard for the other person to do, or if it affects their children, that you are the mean stepparent, even if you know in your heart that you are doing the right thing for their lives. Change is never easy in anyone's life, but I was so concerned about this child living a life of being negative and falling into a deep depression the way things were going. I was also afraid it would ruin his life, and his ability to fit into society.

Matt was also very heavy, which did not help his self-esteem. He was not made to eat anything he did not want to, so his diet consisted of meat, potatoes and sweets. All this weight and his constant withdrawal from everyone and everything had taken its toll on his self image, and it was very low at this point in his life. So he would sit day after day in the corner and read, and get deeper and deeper into himself. He never got any exercise to help with his weight problem.

I could see another discussion was in order, because I was still concerned about his life and attitude, so we had another meeting and I suggested that things had to change regarding eating and exercise and chores around the farm, which I knew would be good for him. I could see the pain again in Frank's eyes, as he realized the problem had to be dealt with. Being strict and setting down rules for Matt was tough for him because it was something that he had not done before. I suggested that maybe he needed an outside project, now that we were on the farm, to get him out of the corner reading everyday and get some exercise to help his physical appearance and have him get some fresh air. I hoped this would help him feel better about himself and feel better about his life before school started again in the fall.

So we decided that everyone was to be assigned duties, it would be good for everyone and there was always plenty of things to be done around the farm. I also suggested that we start a policy for everyone about eating because I had become a short-order cook, this one didn't like this and the other one didn't like that. The new policy would be: When the food was passed around the table at meal time, each person would try a small portion of each item that was passed before them and eat it. If they didn't help themselves they were given a larger portion by us to eat.

Boy, what a struggle we had on our hands when this started taking place, and I know it was very hard on my husband especially since he had let Matt do as he pleased for such a long time at the table, just trying to meet his emotional needs in every way. But we worked in a cooperative manner and each child had his or her struggles with the new policies. But the main thing was we were united on our decision and that saved our sanity and our marriage. We made it work for us. We have tried lots of things, but there is no way to make it work, except being united in all your decisions, and sticking together no matter what. Hang on tight when the hurricanes come through your lives.

One of the hardest thing we had to face was the kids plotting one of us against the other. Of course his kids would go to him to ask permission to do something and mine would come to me, which was only the natural thing for them to do. We could see we had to have another summit meeting and have an understanding of how to handle this, because it was driving a wedge between us and driving us crazy.

We then made a pact that when a child came to one of us with a decision to be made or asking to do something, we would not say yes or no until we had talked it over in privacy. So each time there was a decision to be made we would meet and talk it over in privacy and no one outside knew how this decision was reached. As soon as a decision was reached, we would come out united again, hanging on to each other and giving our ultimate steadfast decision. No matter how much crying and opposition there was to the decision, we would not waiver from our decision. After much carrying on, they soon discovered that they had to accept our united decisions, because we were not going to change it or give in to anyone.

This was probably one of the keys to our success in putting our families together. You have to be first in each others lives, and you have to be strong and united in your decision making. I am not saying this is easy, but stick to it, and it will get easier. Of course they tried on many occasions to put us on the spot and ask us to make a hasty decision because so and so was on the telephone and needed to know right now. But the answer was, "No, not until we discuss this and make the decision will any answer come. You will have to call your friend back." Eyes would roll, but that was the way it was.

When we made decisions together, I believe we made better decisions for their lives based on more facts and not being hasty. This way it did not pull our relationship apart. It built a stronger and more united marriage and we learned to communicate well. I feel it was better for the children because they never saw us fight over any decision we made about them, and it gave them more basis not to get in the middle of our relationship.

The kids were busy with the farm, changing water, fixing fences and trying to weed the garden. Lots of times it was weeding *the plants*, because they weren't too concerned whether it was a weed or a plant, but they tried in their own ways.

10

A HARD PROBLEM TO FACE

It was time for my youngest daughter to start school. She was a beautiful loving child and was very creative. She loved sitting on Frank's lap and stroking his soft hair and sucking her thumb, and he even let her braid his short hair and put ribbons in the braids on several occasions. They grew very close and loved each other very much.

She began school and was having such a difficult time trying to learn to read. I would spend lots of evenings trying to help her, but she would become so frustrated trying and I would get so frustrated thinking she just wasn't trying to learn her reading.

About halfway through the year, she still couldn't read. She was feeling so stupid and so dumb, and of course all the kids would laugh as she would stumble through the lines and try to read when it was her turn. I knew she must have some serious problems, but where do I start to help her?

I went to the school nurse and she referred me to the school's traveling counselor and I found out they had a person who came around once a month to test children that seemed to have a problem. I made an appointment with her for my daughter to be tested so we could try and help her. After testing her, they found out she had some severe learning disabilities and dyslexia. She also did not hear any vowel sounds. It was serious and extremely hard for her to learn like other children.

My next questions was, "Where do I get help for her so she can learn to read?" There was a college in a nearby town not far away that had a program to help kids with her problems. After reviewing her case, they sent her to a special teacher who was being trained in this college to work with kids with her problems. Everyday as she went to her special teacher, she felt even more inadequate because she felt she was different from the other kids, and the progress was very slow and discouraging for her.

Reading disabilities have become better understood now, which can help a child at an early age get help and understanding. If I had had any previous experience with these sort of problems, I would have been able to recognize that she had some serious problems before she started school, and could have gotten her help sooner.

Some of her disabilities were trouble with balance, it took her grandfather two weeks to teach her to skip. She could never really learn to tell time. When I would have her write her letters, she would always make her D's and B's back to back, because she never knew which way they were supposed to go. When you had her copy a sign, like a stop sign, to practice her letters she would write it on a piece of paper as pots, instead of stop. She was sure that she had spelled it correctly because that was they way she would see things, so that was the way she copied them down.

I also went to a special class that was put on for parents. They gave you a sheet of typed letters that were written the way your child would see the letter through his or her eyes when they read it. I took one look at this sheet of letters, some letters were backwards, and some were spelled backwards and a lot of the lines were at different levels that did not follow in straight lines. I had difficulty deciding where all the letters were supposed to go and even trying to figure out if I was seeing them right or wrong. Trying to sort it all out was very difficult. I took one look at this typed sheet and, as I studied it, I realized what my child was going through in some small way, but I did not have to face this everyday like she did.

She would call me from school when she was trying to find her school bus, not knowing if the number on the bus was 12 or 21, and not sure if she was seeing it right or wrong. She was very confused at which bus she was supposed to get on to come home everyday. Life was very hard for this pretty, little girl.

This is not caused by poor eyesight or low intelligence, but the brain does not process information in the proper order. In lots of instances, this is inherited through families, and many people do not recognize it because in lots of cases kids learn to compensate for their problems at an early age.

She spent a lot of years in special training, but it really takes its toll on their self-esteem and self-worth. The counselor told me that they are very high-IQ children and very smart in lots of ways, but this blockage in their brain inhibits them to read or retain anything they read. They are so busy trying to figure out what and how to read the things they read, that they have nothing left to help them retain what they are reading. She never could pass a test or memorize anything, which has made school and life very hard for her, and has caused a lot of stress in her life. She has tried so many things and failed that her life has been so hard for so long. It is so frustrating as a parent, because you can do so little to help them, and everything they try is so difficult for them.

I encourage anyone who thinks that their child has any sort of problem, please try to recognize it and get them help as soon as possible. I have seen many parents of children with these problems deny that their child has a problem, and the child suffers their whole life and soon it is too late to help them. They become a delinquent because they feel like such a dumb loser and they have no self-image left. I know what my daughter has lived with even with all the help she has had. She still battles this everyday of her life, and she is a beautiful, bright person with a wonderful personality and tries so hard.

My hope is that I can help one parent of one child understand this problem. I know it is becoming more and more recognized and dealt with than when she was a child. Get them help as soon as possible because there are lots of programs in the schools now to help these children. Remember, it is not anything to be ashamed of so please get your child the help they need.

We finally made the decision to hold her back and have her go through the first grade again. It was terrible when her friends moved on and the guilt of not being able to succeed was there again. I feel she lost most of the first grade and finally had just began to read so taking the first grade over was the best thing for her, rather than waiting until later and not being able to keep up as she went through school with her classmates. It was a hard decision; we discussed it at length and decided we needed to hold her back because it was best for her in the long run, and our feelings now didn't really matter, it was her life that mattered.

11

Disciplinary Action

Those girls, the two older ones were always in trouble. In fact, one day they were very disobedient and didn't come home and didn't call like they knew they were supposed to. We knew things were getting out of hand and they were pushing all they could, like normal kids. So we decided after talking it over that they needed to have disciplinary action, which in our household meant a spanking when they got home. This was the first time Frank had to spank my daughter, Lisa, which was very hard for him. But in my eyes and God's eyes he was the head of the household and it had to be done by him. I knew he loved her and he did it in love, not anger, but it seemed like he was just beginning to get a good relationship with her, but what is love? It's caring enough to discipline and show you care. We both wondered how this would affect their overall relationship. He was very worried about this.

Well, when they finally decided to come home, he took both of them in the other room and talked to them and explained to them what he had to do, and spanked both of them and they cried and he held them and cried with them. I think it was harder on him than the kids, but he knew it was his responsibility to them. With five children, you have to control and you can't lose it or you will lose the whole family to disobedience. You would not have believed the change that came over those girls after the discipline was administered. I guess they knew he cared about them and it was wonderful how they responded, it made you want to spank them everyday.

We came to the conclusion that if you don't discipline a child, they don't know you care for them or love them. They need it for security in their lives to know you care enough to want their lives to turn out and for them to learn to do the right things. God's order is for the man to be head of the household do the disciplining and be united in this with his wife, and realize that it is best for your relationship. The children benefit from a united love and they need to learn God's order for the family. We took refuge in God's plan. He created the institution of marriage and family, so it is not surprising, therefore, that his guidelines on authority and the family work so well. In the book of Proverbs (23:14), it is written, *"Do not withhold discipline from a child, if you punish him with the rod, he will not die, punish him with the rod and save his soul from death."* We also put our trust in, *"Train up a child in the way he should go and when he is old he will not depart from it"* (Proverbs (22:6).

Relinquishing discipline to the father, for a great number of parents, is very hard especially when you put children together, you have to trust that person to let him punish your child, especially mothers. It was at times hard for me to relinquish this authority to Frank, but I knew that he loved them and did not do it in anger. This was a real learning experience for both of us, but the change in attitudes and respect from the girls was amazing.

It was harder for Frank to let go and let me correct his children. I always felt tenseness in my husband when I would try and discipline his two children, so I was careful not to do that too much. He had developed such a need to protect them, that it had become so automatic that he couldn't control it. I did not want to hurt him, which was very difficult, and we were only able to talk about it years later. It was too painful at the time and later we realized it was not good for the children, because they needed the input from a woman in their lives.

Many times I was on a guilt trip because I wasn't being what he wanted me to be to his children, but I couldn't get past those protective instincts he had built up. I would not say anything until I could not take it anymore, and then I was usually really mad, which was my nature anyway to let things build up, but it was not good for any of us. This caused me a lot of health problems. I was in the hospital with colitis caused by nerves on many occasions trying to get my health back. Later on, I began retreating from his two children so as not to get involved, and it hurt everyone.

I am sorry to this day this happened, because I don't think they were ever sure where they stood with me, and how I cared for them. The thing they needed the most, a woman's love and touch and understanding, was taken from them by a father who loved them, but couldn't let go of certain things that were almost uncontrollable for his nature.

As summer progressed, we decided to get the kids some bottle calves and have the kids feed them to teach them more responsibility. This would also get Matt out more often and all the kids would develop an interest in animals. The TV was a constant battlefield and we needed some wholesome distractions. It takes time to change things, you have to remember that, and not get discouraged and give into the kids. Many times we wanted to surrender and look away when there was a particular program we didn't approve of, but we would not have done the best thing for the children.

We got each child a calf, this was a real neat experience for them, and they enjoyed it. Although the mess in the utility room of mixing calf bottles and the mud from the barn was horrendous, I felt it was worth it to see what the children all learned from having their own calf. The calves would follow them around bawling, thinking they were their mothers, sucking on their fingers and chasing them around with the empty bottles after the milk was gone.

One morning when the children went out to feed the calves, Dale came running in yelling, "My calf is dead!" This was a real blow to the kids and it was too late in the season to get another calf to replace it, so it was a sad day for everyone. I guess on the farm you see the good, the bad and the ugly. It is hard on the kids to lose their pets, but unfortunately it happens and you have little control over hurts like this.

12

PLEASE BE SPECIFIC

Frank had come up with the idea to leave the kids instructions everyday, written-out ones that they would be accountable for. I need to explain a little about Matt, so you will fully understand what and why the following happened.

He was a very intelligent boy, but unfortunately he had no common sense. You had to be very specific with directions or you were in trouble, as we soon found out.

One morning in particular, Frank sat down and wrote out his instructions for the jobs that Dale and Matt were responsible for. Matt's instructions read: *Put the hose in the garden*, because the weather had been hot and the garden was looking very dry. Well, Frank went to work that day and at the end of the day as he drove in the driveway and looked over at the garden, there was no water running anywhere, and it looked like no water had been running there all day. He came into the house and called for Matt. He asked, "Why isn't the water running in the garden? I gave you specific instructions that you were to water the garden."

Matt picked up his list of instructions and pointed out that it said: *Put the hose in the garden*, exactly what he did, he had followed the instruction correctly. He looked perplexed as his father said, "Why didn't you turn the water on?"

Matt was still looking rather confused and replied, "Oh you didn't tell me to turn the water on just to put the hose in the garden...."

Frank let out a sigh, and decided at that point he had to be more specific with his instructions. So the next couple of days he decided to try again. Matt's instructions said: *Please mow the lawn.* Now, that doesn't seem to be one of the instructions you have to go into detail about....or does it? He felt good about these instructions for the day and went off to work humming a happy tune.

I was busy in the house, it seemed like cook and decide what to cook was all I did to keep all these mouths fed. There were always hungry eyes looking at me saying, "What's for lunch? What's for supper?"

Matt was continually knocking on the back door trying to finish his duties, first it was, "Where is the lawn mower?" Then it was, "It won't start."

I suggested checking the gas.

"Where is the gas?" was the next question.

"In the barn," I told him, and it went on and on for awhile.

I looked at this intelligent boy and just shook my head. His father had said this was an easy task, just mowing the lawn. I continued working in the kitchen and was relieved when I finally heard the lawn mower going. Not paying any attention to what was going on, just relieved that things were finally moving before his dad came home.

Later, I heard Frank drive in the yard. I felt good knowing the lawn was finally done, and he would be so happy that the chores were done. But as he got closer to the house, he could see the lawn was mowed, but what was all that plastic laying around the yard? Oh, no! It was the hoses that had been left lying out on the lawn.

You know the question. "Why are all the hoses chopped up? And why weren't they picked up before the lawn was mowed?"

Again, "You didn't tell me to pick up the hoses..."

Here we go again. Can you believe this kid has a brain, and a good one at that? This was a couple of days after Dale's calf had died, so the next morning Frank sat down to write out more instructions for that day. Matt's instructions were: *Bury the calf.*

Frank left for work, but I noticed he was gone just a short time and he came roaring back into the driveway and ran into the house and sat down at the list. I asked him what was wrong. He said he had been driving down the road to work and began wondering what could go wrong today with the list he had left, and suddenly he got this vision of what had gone wrong the past weeks with his instruction and decided that he had to come back home and be more explicit with his instructions. He shared with me the thoughts he had about the instructions of burying the calf, and seeing Matt digging the hole and dragging a live calf to the hole to be buried. He wasn't going to take any chances this time on leaving very clear instructions. He sat there a minute, and behind the instructions he left, he put in-parenthesis: *(the dead calf)*. Then he left again with a smile, knowing that when he came home that afternoon, things would be done right and there would not be any mistakes with his instructions.

What a relief that day when he came home. Things were done right. He sat down at the table with a sigh, believe me it was never dull in this household. We had started a policy that when he came home after work we would sit down and spend at least a half-hour talking together. This was our special time for just the two of us, and the kids at first had a hard time leaving us alone, even for a short period, but soon they came to understand that they were not to interfere with this special time we had together.

It was great. We shared our day's joys and frustrations, and to this day we still spend this special time together. It is so important that you take time for the two of you, because time has a way of getting gobbled up by everyone and everything around you. Don't feel guilty about it and make other people respect your time together. It is very important for your communication skills and your marriage.

Within the next few days, Lisa's calf was dead. We were very worried that we would lose all the calves, but we managed to keep the other two isolated and they didn't die. We needed to get them off the bottle because we had planned a trip to North Dakota before school started to meet Frank's family. So we all agreed that the two remaining calves would be sold when they were old enough and the profits would be split between the four kids.

The calves were growing very fast and were able to start eating soon on their own, so we would be able to leave someone in charge of feeding them and they wouldn't have to worry about bottles. They were real pets and loved the kids and would follow them everywhere. Matt and his calf grew very close, and it was a wonderful companion for him, he would even ride it all over the farm, and she would come up behind you and lick you with her big tongue if you were out in the pasture with her. This experience was a good one in spite of the losses and frustrations.

13

OUR FIRST TRIP

We decided to take a trip to meet Frank's folks in North Dakota, but as usual we were trying to figure out how we would lodge and be able to feed everyone on our budget, which was tight and still be able to enjoy this trip. We came up with an idea to buy a camp trailer for our trip, and the money we saved on meals and hotels would help pay for our trailer and we would have something at the end of the trip to enjoy as a family and take other vacations with it at a later date.

We finally found a reasonable one, of course it was in need of some repairs. It fit our budget and it was cheap, but we were used to fixing things up and getting by with them. The people that owned it had hit something sticking up on the road, or a curb, and had torn all the plumbing loose underneath the trailer. But being a plumber, Frank knew how to fix this problem, so we purchased the trailer and when we finished with the repairs, it was as good as a new one and ready for a trip.

The day we decided to leave finally came and we loaded and loaded for days and it seemed that everyone had taken plenty of things. I think we had everything we would possibly need for six months or so. We were all loaded up with the five kids and all their possessions, and headed out on our first vacation, a new journey to North Dakota. I never figured out why they call them vacations, I was worn out by the time we left.

We had put a canopy on our pickup earlier so that worked out well. The kids loaded their games, snacks and sleeping bags in the canopy that would be their little territory for the trip. This was an ideal arrangement for all of us and we loaded the kids in the back and we jumped in the front seat, shut the window between us and the kids, and off we went.

We stopped at parks on the way which were very enjoyable and it allowed everyone to get some exercise, then we would have lunch and this helped break up the trip for everyone. After an hour or so, we would load up and be off again for our journey.

At times, we kept driving with much confusion in the back canopy, but as long as no one was dying we kept driving, hoping they would settle their differences, because it seemed no matter where they were they would be fighting over something or someone had looked at them the wrong way or touched something they owned. You know the story.

A couple of times a day we would stop for beverages and gas, depending on how everyone controlled their drinking habits. They each saved some of their own money to buy a few things each time we stopped. Usually Dale would spend all his money the first few days, while

Matt wouldn't buy anything. He would never spend any money and then he would try and mooch off everyone else, then the fight would start. Seven of us in a camp trailer for that long was a challenge, and it began raining after the second day on the road so everyone was more confined when we stopped.

We all got on each other's nerves, but it was especially trying when we would stop and I tried to cook lunch and everyone is sitting and moving around the trailer where I was trying to prepare the meals and keep things halfway in order. At times, I thought I must be crazy for considering this a vacation, especially when we would sit down and eat a meal. Everyone would begin complaining, especially Matt, who didn't like anything and didn't want any mayonnaise or butter on anything he ate.

When we arrived it was a beautiful day and the sun was finally shining again. Frank's folks had a cabin on the lake so the kids could go out there and spend time in the water and have fun, and water ski behind the boat which they all enjoyed. This helped release some energy so they let up on each other and stopped picking at each other. We had a great time there and his folks were very accepting and loving to all the children. You couldn't even tell which ones were their real grandchildren and they were very loving, caring people, which made it easy to love them.

We had a marvelous time, but we knew the time was drawing near to get on the road again. Another three days on the road, but we loaded up again and started home. Somehow we made it without many casualties. We finally arrived home with a lot of work to catch up on, of course there was the garden and its weeds and the weeds were higher than the plants. The pasture water needed to be changed and lots of things had to be done to get ready for fall. We also had cattle that had to be taken to the market to be sold to make our payment.

Oh, and then there was school to consider, and we were not at all ready for that. Matt had changed the most. He looked so nice and slim to start this school year, he had slimmed down a few pants sizes and none of his clothes fit. Keeping him busy and the outside work along with chores and changing sprinklers and eating right had changed him so much in just one summer.

With him slimming down and the other children taking growth spurts, we discovered that none of their clothes fit, which meant lots of planning and some trips to the store before school started.

I was dreading a shopping day, because of the cost and trying to get everyone outfitted would not be easy.

One day I got up full of energy and decided that I had better go for it before I lost my courage to take them all shopping. So off we headed, I figured we might as well get it over with all at once.

Wrong!

Five kids school shopping and each one wanting me to look at this and see how this looked when they began trying things on was insane. It seemed like whenever we went shopping or camping, Matt would always get lost and we would spend a lot of time looking for him, and everyone would be mad at him because he wouldn't show up at the designated time and place like everyone else. Lisa always got mad if she didn't get everything she wanted and would punish us for a week and not talk (this is punishment?). It was great.

Anyway I came home with a whopper of a headache, and a tired body and tired kids. My husband came home from work, and took one look at me and said, "let's go out for supper." Boy did I need that. I didn't know where we were going to come up with the money for supper, but at that point I didn't care. Of course we had to go through a small confrontation about taking Matt with us, because he never had any outings, my husband thought he needed to have a social outing with us. This time it did not go over at all, and I finally convinced him we really needed this time for just the two of us alone and that I had been with the kids all day and needed a break from them.

It was hard on him leaving Matt behind, but he really knew that it was best, and his protective nature still wanted to help Matt be happy. It really affected our relationship. I became very resentful of him wanting to take him everywhere we went. I guess that was understandable on both our parts, but you always get the guilt and the WOS feeling (wicked old stepparent) when you say no. We finally got away and had a nice evening alone, which we both so desperately needed.

School seemed to go pretty well and everyone was involved in activities, which meant back and forth evening after evening from town. If you have a family, you know what I mean. Everyone has to be at a different place at a different time.

One evening as we were talking, we realized that we were going to have to do something to have some privacy in our own home. We had to make a decision soon to try and find a place where we could be alone and have another bathroom available. We all had to get ready at the same time in the morning and the bathroom became a war zone. I don't know how people did it years ago with big families, I guess they had outhouses that helped with the congestion.

Matt was not happy at school He had not made any friends and would not participate in any school activities. We had a summit meeting and decided that we must, for his sake, insist that he join in some school activities and belong somewhere among his classmates. So we checked out the school activities and when we knew something was coming up that we thought would be good for him to participate in we would say, "OK, you get ready you are going." We would drive him to the school activity, and then sit there and fight with him to get him out of the car to join in the school activity with the other kids. It was really hard going through this time with him crying as we drove him to the school activity, and us practically having to drag him in the school to attend the activity. But we knew that we had to do it if he was going to have a well adjusted life or any life at all with the human race. This was hard on me, being the initiator and his father having to go along with this. Even if he knew it was the best for him, it was still hard. Finally, our persistence paid off and he began coming out of his shell and actually started enjoying the people and the activities he was participating in.

The older girls were different. They would be involved in anything and everything. It got so that we would only allow them to be involved in one or two activities a week. One evening, I made nine trips to town after 5:00, six was a normal evening. It was very exhausting, but we knew they had to be active and enjoy being part of the school activities.

14

OUR BLUE HEAVEN

We had discussed our need for privacy and had been planning for quite a time to find a place for just the two of us to share our times together, a bedroom and a bathroom. But there were always so many other priorities that we kept putting it on the back burner. We were at our wits end with no privacy from the 10 eyes that followed us everywhere, watching everything we did. So we finally made a decision to find an answer to our problem. We searched the outside and the inside of our house to try and figure out how we could find a corner for us to have some privacy.

One day, Frank came home with an idea. He said "Let's check the attic and see what we can come up with up there." So we crawled up in the attic, and came up with an idea for our dream space. We decided that we could add a bedroom and a bathroom on top of our house, just for us. It would give us privacy and we would have another bathroom, and that way we could save on building expenses because we did not have to have a foundation for another building since we were adding to the top of our house. We did think of a rope ladder we could pull up when we wanted complete privacy, but decided to put in a staircase instead.

We began drawing up our plans to begin the project. We were so excited about our idea and spent lots of time planning and working on our own place, our dream was finally becoming a reality. Everyone was interested in the project and what was going on up on the roof. We began ripping the roof off the building, not even thinking about getting a building permit or anything else preliminary to starting a building project. The next day we received a stop work order from the local building department. We suddenly realized in our excitement we had forgotten one important step, we needed to get a building permit before we proceeded with our plan.

One afternoon when Lisa and Debbie got home from school, they decided to investigate what was going on up there. They crawled up the ladder and were looking over our new addition, when all of a sudden as I was downstairs working in the kitchen, I heard a crashing noise. As I looked up in the hall, there was Lisa hanging through the ceiling with two legs hanging below the ceiling, suddenly there was a body attached to those legs coming through and soon she came flying through the ceiling and crashed to the floor. There was nothing anyone could do but watch her fall. It was one of those things you wanted to laugh at, but you weren't sure how much the person was hurt, and how upset they would be if you laughed.

The main thing was that she wasn't hurt, beyond scratches, so we were thankful for that. The girls had learned a valuable lesson about walking up there and how to be careful where to walk, and to stay on the boards and not walk in between them on the weak sheetrock that would not hold their weight. Luckily, where she fell through was going to be where we were going to cut the ceiling open for our stairway. So it didn't do much damage to the project and its progress, just another hole. We didn't have enough room for a regular stairway, so we decided to put in a spiral staircase. Later, we found out it was really interesting getting anything into that room that was very wide or heavy, because the stairway went round and round on a pole and was a very narrow passage way.

About four months later, we were finally ready to move in. What a job it had been, but we knew it would be worth it as we pounded every nail and stood up the walls. We were so excited we would finally have a place where we could be alone and have our own toothbrush and shaver and even our own comb. That seemed to be something that would always disappear and turn up missing the most, and no one ever seemed to have it or admit to have taken it, it was just gone.

That first evening when we were finally finished, we ran up the stairway and shut the door behind us and locked it. We each let out a big sign of relief, some privacy at last. We had a sliding glass door in our room with a beautiful view of the mountains, and also this door gave us access to move furniture in which was quite a task. We had to lift all our furniture up by ropes on the deck and then bring it through this door, because of the limitations with our stairway. We had our cabinets built in the room which helped the moving process. These cabinets were great, we could store all the things we wanted to keep for just us. What a change this was going to be for us, to have goodies and anything else we could not keep in the house all to ourselves in our own room.

We were all snuggled in, enjoying our blue and white bedroom. That is why we called it our Blue Heaven. Suddenly, as we were enjoying ourselves and our privacy, we heard a noise outside our glass sliding door on the deck. As we looked out, we saw five bodies appearing on our deck outside our bedroom sliding glass door. I could not believe it, my husband had left the ladder sitting alongside the house after we finished moving in and guess what? The kids had pushed the ladder up to the deck and climbed up on our deck, and they were all standing on the deck looking into our Blue Heaven. I am sure they were curious, and could not stand the thought that we were finally alone, and they weren't included in whatever was going on in our private location. They were not used to not being included.

I don't want to tell you my thoughts at this time. I broke down and started crying. "Will we ever be alone?!" I shouted.

I looked up at my husband and said, sort of kiddingly, "Go push them off the deck." I think I really felt like I meant it at the time, I was so upset. The kids could see how upset I was so they climbed down the ladder the way they had come up. We then had a talk with the kids about this situation and decided we would have to have a talk with them about our privacy and what it meant when we were in our room and wanted to be alone, just the two of us. They were instructed that they needed to knock when the door was closed and it was to be locked when we were not at home. It was the only way to maintain our privacy, and our sanity, and keep our comb.

This room was our salvation and helped save our marriage. Many times we made important decisions behind those closed doors.

We were also both so thankful we had made this decision to go ahead with this project, and glad we had worked so hard to finish it. We found out it is very important that you have a place of your own, and that the children know that this is your private place. It helps them realize that grown-ups need their time alone, and it is really necessary for a good relationship to develop between you and your husband. It also helped to have a private place where we could talk about problems with the children and arrive at answers without the children hearing what was going on.

We learned that we needed some time together, because we could not afford to go out to get privacy. So we set aside evenings to make dates with each other and that has worked well throughout our marriage, and we still do it today. You have to take time and plan your times together or you never get around to any time just for the two of you, because of all the family priorities that usually come first. We, to this day, block off Wednesday and Friday evenings on our busy calendars each month and make it a point of never missing our date nights together.

Sometimes when we didn't have any money to spend to go out, we would just spend the evening together walking and talking or just getting an ice cream cone.

After we finished our Blue Heaven, we had a little table and chairs up there in front of the window and we would have a candlelight dinner up there alone. We had many special evenings in our Blue Heaven. We decided that we would plan our special dates, and we would take turns planning what we would do for the evening so that we could use our own ideas of what we each enjoyed doing.

I remember one date night in particular I planned. I fixed a nice candlelight dinner in our Blue Heaven and served dinner in a skimpy teddy nightgown. Of course he liked that, and then we spent the entire evening there alone. It was a really special time for the two of us.

The next date, it was my husband's turn to plan what he would like to do that evening. I waited with anticipation at what I visualized in a woman's eyes that our date would be like. I rushed home from work that evening with all kinds of special thoughts of what a romantic evening we were going to have. When I got home from work he was nowhere to be found, so I assumed that he was making his plan up in our Blue Heaven. I couldn't stand the suspense any longer, so I ran up the staircase, excited to see what we were going to do on our date this evening. I hadn't learned yet that a man's idea of a romantic evening and a woman's idea could be so different.

I opened the door to our bedroom and didn't see Frank anywhere in the room. I shut the door behind me and out jumped my husband from behind the door where he was hiding. He grabbed me from behind and tackled me and escorted me to the bed. I looked at him in surprise, and said "Aren't we going to eat first?" Not realizing his idea of a date yet at this point, we were on the bed and both looking startled, him by my comment and me from this surprise date not at all like I had visualized. `We looked at each other again and both started laughing. Thank goodness we could both laugh about this. We both realized at the same time how different men and women are in their attitudes about what is important on a date.

To this day, we joke about our dates. I will look at him and he will say, "I know we have to eat first." Women and men have to realize that there is such a difference in the way women visualize your times together and the way a man looks at something exciting for him. You have to be able to talk about this and discuss your frustrations with each other and come to some kind of an understanding of each other's needs. Sometimes the other mate has not met up with your expectations when things don't happen the way our minds have planned them. You have to realize that this isn't selfishness, it is just the way our brains work. So be able to laugh about it and discuss it, and be ever so patient with one another's feelings and needs.

15

PARTING WITH YOUR PET IS NEVER EASY

The time had come for Matt's cow to be sold, she was a nice 1000-pound Holstein heifer by now, and we would need to find a dairy to sell her to, to complete her life cycle. She was a beautiful cow, but as far as she was concerned, she was still a calf. She would follow Matt around out in the pasture, and come up behind him and want to be scratched and lick him with her big tongue. She loved for him to ride her around the farm. She was a real pet.

One afternoon, we were all out in the pasture playing baseball and all of a sudden I felt this big, sticky thing on my back. It scared me, but then I realized it was just our affectionate calf. It was hard for him to think about parting with her, but one of our friends took her for his dairy herd. Matt was able to go see her several times after that. Finally, they both adapted to the changes in their lives and the last time he went to see her she did not acknowledge him at all.

It was sad, but we were glad she had a good life and had finally became a real cow. It was easier because the other calves were sold for meat. The one we put in the freezer we had named him Sirloin, so when we talked about him at meals, it would not seem as cruel as saying Sam or Harry. Especially if we had company we would talk about Sirloin and it seemed easier for everyone to handle and not so personal.

Matt was growing up. He had made a decision to make the army academy his career. This decision has to be made before you enter your sophomore year of High School so you can take the classes to prepare you for West Point. He had a lot of hard work ahead of him, but he always played with his soldiers when he was young and dreamed of being a general with strategies of combat moves. He did this for hours with all his tanks and solders lined up for battle. So I guess this is how he developed his interest in serving in the army. It was getting easier to get him out among people and he even began having friends and participating in activities all by himself. It was great.

We were very disturbed by the influence of the TV in our home, and it seemed that it was a constant battle. The kids were only supposed to watch certain programs at certain times, but we always had to oversee what was going on, and when we were not home we worried about what they were watching. No one was getting their chores done and if any of them had homework, sometimes it was neglected for a TV program, or it was hurried through so they could watch a particular program. We talked about this for quite awhile and then we made a decision to get rid of the TV in our home.

16

A HARD DECISION

We were so frustrated with my oldest son Dale. He was at a very hard age and he had missed so much school with his leg surgery, it had put him so far behind he could not catch up. He was losing interest in being in school and had a very low self-image from his relationship with his father, which did not help him in anyway with his frustrating life. I was getting calls from the school regularly that he was not in class, he would be off fixing someone's car or just off doing his own thing. I knew he was becoming involved with drugs, his personality had changed too much and everyone was always missing money in the house.

It had become an intolerable way for all of us to live, and we knew we had to do something before it ruined our home, and all the children's lives. He was a terrible influence on the other children and we could not let this continue in our home. This was a very painful time for me as I watched things go from bad to worse and had so little control over him and his actions.

We had a summit meeting and talked about what we could do, and we could not come up with a solution that was easy. The choices were all hard, and we realized we had to confront him with the problems and tell him he would have to change his ways or leave our home. This decision nearly killed me, but I knew there was no other way to ever have peace in our home again. We had tried everything else we could think of so we had to confront him. He became very angry and upset and began saying terrible things to us. It was a very bad scene to deal with, but we had to tell him he had to straighten up and abide by our rules or he would have to leave our home, because we could not condone these actions in our home. Our family was finished putting up with his behavior and his yelling and screaming at all of us.

So, in a rage, he threw his clothes in his backpack and got on his bicycle and headed down the driveway. We both wanted with all our hearts to run after him and call him back, not knowing what faced him as he rode off to be in this cruel world by himself, but we knew in our hearts we couldn't do that.

This was one of the hardest things I had to face in my life. He was so young and too young to be on his own and as a mother they still seem like your babies. He was very strong willed and had his own ideas about life and living so all we could do was pray for him at this point and hope that he would wake up and realize that he should come home and abide by the rules to live with us in harmony. My stomach was sick and I was to the breaking point with grief, but there were no easy answers to this solution at this point, and this was the only way.

The summer seemed very long and my nerves were very bad. I tried hard to get a handle on what was going on, but ended up in the hospital again with nerves. Trying to recover from a bout with colitis which always took me sometime to recover and gain my strength again. You feel so helpless and I had no way to help him or know what was going on in his life, or if he was OK. I knew the best thing to do was pray for him, but it seems so small to a mother's heart. I prayed that God would keep him safe, no matter how deep in a pit he got.

I checked with his grandparents and his dad each week, and he finally showed up at his grandparents for part of the summer. It helped some to at least know he was not on the streets hungry or in danger.

These were hard times for us, but I guess no one is spared from that when you have teenagers. It is life and living. But one good thing was that Frank and I were still in love and we knew if we would just persist all this would pass, but our love would endure and that was always utmost in our thoughts each day.

I had not heard from my son for quite awhile and fall was approaching and then one afternoon as I was sitting home a dear couple we knew came by to see me. They were special friends of ours and they had come by because they had a message for me. They told me that during the time they were praying for us, God told them that I would be hearing from my son soon, and that he was OK. That was pleasing for me to hear, and I hoped it would really happen. I knew how stubborn he was, but I knew many people had been praying for him, and for us, and I knew prayer worked. It was a very uplifting message and I thanked them for coming by with this word of encouragement.

I thought in my mind, *I wonder how long it will be until I hear from him,* and waited for that telephone to ring and hear Dale's voice on the other end. They left, and as I shut the door the telephone was ringing, I didn't think anything about it I just answered it and the voice on the other end was my son, Dale. What a blessing.

He paused after he said "Hi, Mom," and said, "I need to talk to you about something." He said, "I want to come home and I will try and live by your rules and make it work for all of us." Talk about joy and prayers answered! I never thought I would see that day come that he would give in and try again. I told him Frank and I would talk it over, I wanted to say "Yes, yes, yes," but I knew the rules not to make any decisions without talking it over with each other. So I told him I would call him back that evening after Frank and I had talked it over and came to an agreement. We talked and agreed to let him try again. We called him back and invited him back into our home, provided that he could follow the rules of our home and keep things peaceful at home.

When he arrived it was a wonderful day, I suddenly knew how the prodigal son's father felt when he saw his son come home. He had weighed heavy on both of our minds since the day he left. His attitude seemed changed and it was even nice to have him home once again.

With school starting, the work was mounting around the house so we made a decision to assign duties of the household work to everyone. With me working, I was never caught up and it helped if everyone was more conscious of what needed to be done around the house. Two would take turns washing the dishes and two would fold the clothes and put them away. One would pick up the house. These duties were all assigned and I was not to nag them about their chores. If they were not done all I had to do was tell Frank, and he would deal with the children's responsibilities and see that they were done.

This helped me a lot and took some of the burden off of me that I had to deal with. It went pretty good considering, and it helped me so much with my work load. The kids began to learn responsibility and how to help around the house. It was a good lesson for everyone no matter if they were a boy or girl. They needed to learn what it takes to keep a household running.

17

TEENAGE REBELLION

Boy, we had plenty of teenage rebellion. There were so many frustrating times, and many times I did not handle it very well. When I think back, which I know doesn't do anyone any good, I am ashamed sometimes the way I thought, or how I reacted to certain things that happened. But there is so much pressure on you and you are trying so hard and there is always at least three kids mad at you at one time, and you are trying to do what's best for everyone. It is a difficult task.

Lisa was developing a very stand-off attitude. We had been through months of treats from her, and it was, "If you don't let me do this or that, my dad will let me and I will go live with him."

This is natural. I have talked with many parents since then, that have experienced the same problem. Of course the grass is always greener on the other side, until they get to the other parent's home and of course they aren't usually happy with that situation either. A lot of it is the age, and no matter how you try, things are difficult for everyone.

We were becoming worn down from all these threats, and we knew they were not good for either of us. Something had to be done soon because we could not put up with this any longer. So we decided that I would call her father and ask him if I could send her there for awhile to live with him. So things were OK with her father and we packed her up and sent her to live with her father, where she believed everything would be rosy.

I was very nervous sending her there because I did not want her in that volatile atmosphere, which had upset her so much in the past that she could not sleep at night. I felt at this point I did not have a choice because something had to be done. We were not going to put up living with her threats anymore.

So I explained to her that she was going to live with her dad and that she would have to stay there for at least three weeks and then could make a decision on where she was going to live. At that point, she would have to stick to the decision she made for that year and not run back and forth. So off she went feeling very smug. She thought she had won the battle. She was going to have the time of her life and do anything she wanted, so she thought.

She left and I prayed once again that God would keep her safe and help her learn her lessons without too much pain. Boy, mothers spend a lot of time on their knees raising kids. I knew I could lose her forever and the influence we had made on her life, but the stand off had to be made.

Things were pretty quiet for a couple of days and I didn't hear anything from her, but on the third night I got a call from her and she was crying, saying, "I want to come home tomorrow."

I took a deep breath, and said, very calmly, although my insides were screaming, *tell her to come home*, I said, with all the strength I could muster up, "No, you must stay the three weeks. that was our decision, and after that time you then need to make a decision." I knew that her dad would not harm her physically, maybe emotionally, but I knew it had to be done that way. She called several times in those weeks and it nearly broke my heart, but the answer still had to be the same, and it was still, "At the end of the three, long weeks you can make your decision where you are going to live permanently."

The three weeks finally came to an end. She called again and said "I want to come home and make it work." So we agreed to let her come home and talk about an attitude change. She said to me when she got home, "Don't you ever send me there again."

I promptly said, "It's your decision." Things seemed to go a lot better after that. I hoped the power struggle was over and thank goodness we had all won. It is very hard to let them go, but sometimes you have to take the chance of losing them forever. You can't live and survive with blackmail.

I have learned if you want to keep something forever, you have to give it away, no matter what the cost. I have seen parents hold on to their kids so tight and not let them go with the other parent. It becomes almost an obsession with them to be with that other parent, and eventually you end up losing them in the end through hatred for you because you have kept them from the other parent.

Shortly after this, Frank and I had been getting physicals for life insurance coverage that we were applying for, and a nurse had to come to the house to take our applications. We were talking about making our will too and getting things in order. Lisa had overheard us talking about our wills and then we had decided to talk it over with the kids about where they would go if something would happen to us. We were up in our bedroom and shortly after we had talked to the kids, I heard Lisa crying outside our bedroom door. I opened the door and asked her what was wrong, she came in crying and put her arms around Frank and said, "I have to tell you I love you before something happens to you." She put her arms around him and held on tight. We both were in utter shock, she had never shown any affection for anyone, especially Frank. She was very reserved and always kept her feelings to herself.

We both looked at her in amazement and said, "What brought all this on?" She had put together all that we were doing, like making out our wills and the physicals and our talk with them about what would happen to them if something happened to us, and she thought that we were preparing them for something that was about to happen to him. She had never been able to express her feelings to Frank before and she thought he was possibly critically ill. It scared her and she decided she had to tell him her feelings about him before he was gone and it was too late.

It was a very moving time for all of us, and really meant a lot to Frank and to me too as we all stood there with our arms around each other all crying at the same time, both with joy and relief when we assured her everything was fine. It was a healing time for all of us, and it was wonderful for her to express her feelings. This has always been hard and communicating her feelings was never something she did, so this was a big step for her. She would just get quiet and not speak to anyone for days at a time, and would never let anyone know what was really troubling her I don't know if this really helped her with her problem, but it was still a great moment in our relationship. We explained to her all the things that had happened and why they happened, assured her that everyone was going to be OK, and she didn't have to worry, but we complimented her for showing how she felt, which was good.

18

TEACH THEM HOW TO FISH

Spring was back and we decided that it was time for the kids to learn to earn some money and learn the value of working for it. The older four were at the age where they needed to learn to work, so they were all required to get jobs cutting asparagus in the mornings before school. This would give them money for their school activities and clothes, and teach them how to handle money.

Boy, if you have ever taken five kids school shopping, they sure shop differently when it is their own money they have earned rather than your money. They worked very hard and earned a good deal of money cutting asparagus. They all learned to get up in the morning by themselves, they all had alarm clocks and they were each responsible for getting up and getting to work. There would be none of this calling and calling them to get up. That was their responsibility not ours.

I see parents whose children are grown and living at home and they have to plead and beg to get their grown adults up in the morning. Give them an alarm clock when they are young and make it their responsibility for their actions at an early age, this will help them throughout life.

It was rather hectic in the mornings getting them off to cut asparagus, and then having breakfast and getting them off to school. School always started later during asparagus time, so that helped. The children really felt good about themselves earning their own money and had more of the designer clothes they wanted because we only would agree to pay so much on certain specialty clothes they wanted. If they wanted the designer brands, they had to pay the difference. There is no way you can keep the pipeline full when you have four teenagers, and try to keep up with just their needs, not their wants.

When asparagus season was over and summer came, they were all required to get jobs. Lisa began baby-sitting and Debbie started working at a local flower shop part time, and continued all through high school. She would work after school and on weekends. This helped her to buy her own car and when the time came for her to get her driver's license. They each worked and bought their own cars, and maintained them, and had to pay for their insurance coverage. Jobs kept them from getting bored and getting into trouble on the streets with nothing to do.

They were good kids, but kids are always pushing you to the limit. Remember when your kids get mad at you, that you are the parent, they are the children and you have to make decisions for their lives that don't always make them happy. But if you teach them responsibility and how to work, it will help them throughout their lives. My husband always said to me, and to the children too when they complained about work, "You can throw a hungry man a fish, but if you teach him how to fish, he will never be hungry again."

So we tried to teach our children the valuable lessons of fishing for themselves, so they could learn to earn an income and keep a job and become happy, successful individuals. Do it for them, no matter how hard it seems at the time. It is a valuable lesson for them to learn.

19

THE DEMONSTRATION

The activities at school picked up considerably and some evenings there were two and three activities. Of course each child wanted you at his or her activity or program. This was very exhausting and involved lots of planning and running as we tried to attend each event of each child. We knew they were all important, but running from one event to another took its toll on us.

Our grocery bill was the national debt. You couldn't drag in food, toilet paper, shampoo, toothpaste, etc., fast enough for them to use. Of course no one was economical and would think of how much they were using. And hot water, they thought there was no end to it and several times Frank had gone down in the basement and shut the hot water off after a shower had been going for a half-hour at a time. That seemed to be the only solution to get them out of the shower that worked real well, and real fast.

One evening after getting back from the grocery store, Frank went into the bathroom and there was the toilet filled with toilet paper and shampoo spilled in the bathtub. Then and there he decided to have a lesson for everyone on conserving supplies. Being a plumber, the toilet paper seemed of utmost importance, so the lesson was to be on conserving toilet paper. Anyway, when he told me he was going to give a toilet paper demonstration, it really hit me funny. I thought, *I am sure this will help.* I was standing in the background laughing hysterically as I watched him putting on this toilet paper demonstration. He had a roll of toilet paper and was showing them that you only really need three squares. As he folded it neatly, he showed them that this amount of toilet paper should be sufficient to wipe, instead of wrapping it around your hand two or three times and wiping and then throwing this wad in the toilet half a roll at a time. Girls are the worst at this, but I could tell he was really getting through to them by the way the kids were all rolling their eyes, and their concentration was not good at this time. But he was trying, I can't say it made a difference, but it made him feel better anyway.

To this day they still talk about the toilet paper demonstration when they come to visit us. They will look back at Frank as they head for the bathroom and say, "I know, I will only use three squares."

Now Cindy was involved in things too; taking dance, acrobatics and her golden hair was down to her waist. She was missing teeth in front, but was still a darling little girl. She loved her dance and it gave her something to do with her friends and kept her busy so she left the older girls alone, part of the time anyway. She had acquired a new baby pet goat. If you think they are cute and you think you should have one of these darling pets for your kids...*stop*, think again.

She named him Billy. He was darling and he was her constant companion, but he was growing fast. They loved each other and he would go everywhere with her. He had several drawbacks, the worst one was when a car, especially a new one, would drive in the driveway, his favorite trick was to jump up on the car hood and dance on the hood and then jump to the roof where he proceeded to keep dancing. It was impossible to catch him, he was so quick and whenever we heard a car drive in we would try and catch him, but he moved so fast it was impossible.

So we decided we had to build him a pen, but you couldn't keep him in. Everyday he was out again. We kept nailing more and more boards on his pen, but he always found a way to get out. He was really becoming a pest. We put him on a leash, so she could lead him around, but he was getting strong and had a mind of his own about where he wanted to go verses where she wanted to go. He would drag her most of the time, with her screaming and trying to get him to do what she wanted.

One day they had show and tell at school, so she wanted me to bring Billy to school for show and tell. I agreed, but what an experience. I tried to figure out a way to get him to school. I didn't want to take him in the car because I figured that would be too dangerous, so I finally decided to borrow my husband's plumbing van where he could ride in the back, away from the driver. So I finally got him loaded in the van and took off for school. I could hear he was busy all the time I was driving. I could hear him dragging my husband's sacks of screws and nails out of every bin in the back. There were nails and screws flying everywhere, and he loved to eat paper so he would eat the sacks after dumping them. I knew the van must be a disaster by now, but I had to keep driving and I finally made it to school.

What you don't do when you are a mother, but it meant a lot to Cindy to be able to show her pet to her friends.

By the end of school, this goat was getting so unruly that I was really getting embarrassed. So I loaded him back in the van and took him home, wondering what my husband would say about the mess in his van, I didn't know where anything went it was such a mess. I figured the most important thing was to get him home again and worry about it later.

The local parade was the next weekend and guess who wanted to be in the parade. Cindy wanted to take Billy, we had to figure out an outfit for both of them. Of course she was enjoying her dance so much and she had an extra pink ballet costume so we decided that they would each wear one, so we put a pink frilly ballet costume on both of them for the parade. He was getting so strong that he drug her through the parade out of control most of the time, but she had fun and won a prize, and they both looked so cute in their costumes.

Something had to be done with this goat, he was getting too big for her to handle and we could not keep him anywhere. He was in the garden eating, running through the house eating all my houseplants. He would head-butt the screen door in and would come right in the house after Cindy and would get into everything.

Later that month I was having a yard sale, and one of the men that came to the sale was admiring Billy, he asked "Would you sell me that goat?"

Sell him? I would give him away, was the answer I wanted to come up with, but it didn't take me long to answer. I said, "Sure."

He said, "Well, if you can load him in my car, I will buy him."

I didn't ask any questions, like "What are you going to do with him?" I was afraid of what he might tell me and I didn't want to know, because I knew in the back of my mind there were people that like to eat goats. You never saw anyone load a goat so fast in your life. I knew what I was going to face when Cindy got home, but I decided I would let her buy something special she had wanted with the money that would be better company for her than that out-of-control goat.

So when she came home, we talked it over and she decided to get a new doll she had been wanting for quite awhile. For quite some time we didn't dare talk much about Billy, she was sad to see him go. This had been quite an experience, but we were relieved it was over. This cute little baby had become a monster and was only bringing trouble into all our lives.

Two Ballerinas was the title of this entry which featured Cindy and Billy, her goat. They led the parade! Photo by Ardis Emery

20

REMODELING AGAIN

Well, I guess it was time to start another remodeling project. My kitchen was terrible and it had never had any countertops, just contact paper on the plywood, and no cupboard doors. It was indeed unfunctional for all the meals that came out of it. We finally finished the project without too many delays. Boy was it nice working in a new kitchen, I really appreciated it. Our home was really taking shape and after we finished this project, we decided to take a few days and run away together, so we loaded up the trailer and left for a few days. It was great to spend the time resting and have some time together, it helps you face the next crisis.

As we headed home, we were talking about our reactions to things that had gone wrong while we were away before. We realized that we were always getting so upset about whatever happened while we were gone, and we hated to always have to come home to this state of mind and get upset with the kids right away. After all, hey had tried, and they were just kids. This time we decided that we wouldn't get mad and if the cupboards and refrigerator were cleaned out as usual, we would not even get upset, even if there wasn't an egg left. We hummed as we started home, happy with our decision not to get upset this time around.

We drove in the yard with smiles on our faces. As we drove in, we noticed that there were two sprinklers broken off and it looked like Old Faithful blowing up, water shooting everywhere, which meant nothing else was getting watered properly. We noticed our five cows were nowhere in sight. We were still hanging in there at this point, barely.

When we opened the front door, everyone was sitting in the house doing nothing that they were supposed to be doing. We just kept looking at each other and repeating, *We aren't going to get mad.*

We said, "Where are our cows?"

Everyone looked up and finally someone said quietly, "Well, we don't know for sure. You see, remember, you had told us to mow the lawn while you were gone. Well, we came up with this good idea one afternoon that instead of mowing the lawn, we would turn the cows into the yard and let them eat the grass down. We thought it was a great idea at the time, but then we forgot about them being in the yard, and went to bed that night forgetting about them.

"Well, you see, when we got up in the morning to feed them, we could not find them, and we remembered that they were supposed to be in the yard eating grass. They were gone. We searched for them and we couldn't find them."

We were still repeating that we weren't gong to get mad. Well, we did pretty well, except then they got very confident and began thinking they had done such a good job while we were gone.

Then someone made the mistake of saying, "Didn't we do a great job while you were gone?"

Wrong question. We both got mad and we couldn't control ourselves any longer, they had pushed us too far. We explained all the things we were upset about and that we were not happy about the way things had been taken care of. We knew we had to find the cows so we started looking for them, but we didn't have any luck either and we began to think they were lost forever. There went our meat supply we had worked so hard for. Later that afternoon, we were listening to the local radio station and there was a bulletin that someone had found five cows, and to call a certain number and identify them. We knew they must be our cows so we called and sure enough they were, and so off we went to bring them home. At least we would have meat this winter thanks to someone's honesty. Well, anyway, we had a relaxing time away. I guess it was worth it...

21

ANOTHER SUMMER TRIP

Well, we didn't get enough punishment the first time we went on vacation so off we went again with the five kids to North Dakota. We left the key to our gate with a neighbor so he could come in and check things while we were gone. When we were all loaded up ready to leave, we noticed the padlock that we had sitting on the dash to lock the gate as we left was gone. We searched and searched and of course no one knew anything about it. We went back into the house and it was nowhere to be found. After about a half-hour of looking, I happened to turn around and look in the back of the pickup. There was the padlock, locked on the gun rack in the back window of the pickup. Of course no one knew anything about it, so now we were ready to leave and here we had a locked padlock which made it impossible to lock our gate when we left.

So we had to go find our neighbor with the key so we could get the padlock opened and lock the gate before we left, and maybe someday be on our way. We finally found him and got the key and unlocked the padlock and were finally on our way. I could tell this was going to be a good trip.

We always had another person in our midst. That other person's name was, "I didn't do it." He was blamed for everything that went wrong. It was never any of our little angels, they would stick together under any circumstance and not tell on each other.

I had gotten out of the hospital the day before we left, I had been having terrible bouts with colitis brought on by nerves. I still couldn't eat real food after being on intravenous feedings for a few days, and also had a terrible yeast infection. If you have ever ridden in a car in the hot weather for miles with one of these infections, you would understand my plight, which was not fun.

I was really not in the mood to travel and I wanted to jump out of the car several times as we were going down the road, especially when the fighting began. It was, "He's touching me....now he's looking at me..." You know the routine. But I managed to regain my composure and stay in the car, although the pavement looked pretty good at times.

After one day on the road, they all began complaining and wanting to go home, one of them even wanted to take the bus home. We had really tried to make this a fun vacation, but with teenagers I think that is impossible. Every morning we had to stop at a rest area for the girls to get their curling irons hot so they could do their hair, and it usually took about one and a half hours for Lisa to get every hair in place. Frank was fairly patient, but these stops for curling hair wore even his patience thin, but we kept everyone somewhat happy and beautiful and kept going.

The kids needed to stop at a rest area and we were out in the middle of Montana, in the middle of nowhere. We finally found one. They are few and far between out there. They had the chemical toilets in these restrooms and we were not familiar with them. They made these slurping sounds all the time.

Cindy got out to use the restroom and she came running out of the restroom scared to death. She looked up at us so seriously and said, "I am never going into one of these places again. There are poop-eaters in those toilets." When she heard the slurping sounds they were making, she was convinced that there had to be something down that hole. We tried to reassure her, but nothing worked, no rest areas for her again.

We finally reached Helena, Montana. We left the trailer full of kids at Frank's sister's place and went dancing at a local dance place (they are called bars in Montana). We needed some R & R badly at this point, and they always have great music in the little Montana towns. It was a great break for us and we enjoyed ourselves.

Well, I guess we were ready to forge on. As we proceeded that day down the road, we ran into one of those terrible thunder storms that develop there and we even saw a tornado touch down beside the road where we were driving. The wind was terrible and tossed our camper here and there with such force it was hard to stay on the road, but we were afraid to stop. Finally, as we came over a little hill out in the middle of nowhere, we saw a little town in the distance. There wasn't much to this town, but there was a little, white church surrounded by trees. It looked like a shelter from the storm to us, so we headed for that little church as fast as we could.

The storm was so bad it was scary even for me, and the kids were crying from fright. We finally reached the shelter and stayed there during this terrible storm. We could hardly see, the rain was coming down so fast and there was lightning and the wind was blowing terrible. It was a real prairie storm, and not a good experience so far from everything. We all huddled there until we were sure the storm had passed, then we were off again down the road, glad we had found shelter and survived.

We were only about eighteen hours away from our destination so we decided to drive straight through until we got there. We were all tired of traveling and the kids would sleep at night so it made traveling easier. We arrived exhausted, but safe, and had a good night's sleep and we were all ready to go again in the morning, of course the kids were ready to head for the lake to swim, boat and water ski.

They always looked forward to the lake and it was good entertainment for them and made it easier for us to visit with the family. Lots of families were there at the lake with their kids, so they all had a chance to play and frolic in the water together.

Of course the word was out in this small town, that two beautiful blonde girls were in the area, and we had farm boys from everywhere there before we knew it. Going by in boats and driving up in cars, stopping to visit with us, well not us, but the girls.

Never quiet or uneventful when you have teenagers around. Where there are girls, there are boys. They appear out of nowhere. We had a great time and by this time I was able to start eating and was feeling better so we decided to pack up and head home. Cindy got car sick on the way and we would have to stop and let her sit by the road until she felt better.

The weather was hot, but at least there were no storms on our way home.

After a few days we were home again, now to get ready for school again and get caught up on the farm chores once again.

22

THE DATING GAME

Of course kids were coming and going. You never knew how many you were going to have for supper or to spend the night, although we were glad they had their friends in our home, and we knew where our kids were. But it was always like a three-ring circus. With the girls driving, things seemed to get more complicated. Trying to keep track of their activities was a real challenge. I always worried because it seemed that they were always late and in a hurry.

Frank loved to tease the boys who would come to see the girls. He would always ask them their intentions and of course this would embarrass the girls, but he would laugh and had a lot of fun at their expense. We had many kids sit at our table for meals and share how they wished their parents would spend some time with them instead of just giving them money and cars and telling them to go do something, just getting them out of the house. That did not make them happy. They just wanted someone to spend time with them. It was sad.

We tried to spend as much time with our family as we could, we always tried to have some meals together, and tried sharing conversation at meal times together. This is very hard when they are all so busy, but it was a require-ment that we have a few meals together. We dealt with many things in our conversations at the table, and I feel it was quality time spent, and was worth the effort for all of us. As they grew up and left home, never once could any of the kids remember what we had bought for them dur-ing their growing-up years, but they always remembered the time we spent together. So don't feel guilty when you can't give your kids everything, or when you can't buy them everything the other kids have. In the end, it really isn't what matters.

It was very difficult because we were always dealing with 5 personalities, which took so much patience and each child had to be dealt with differently and disciplined differently. We did try and spend time with each child individually, but it was hard to find time for everything with the farm and our business, and the kids' hectic schedules.

Dating really put stress on Lisa and Debbie's relation-ship. They had always been so close. It was the only time since they had first met that they were at odds with each other. They began fighting over boys, Lisa would get a boyfriend and Debbie would flirt with him when he came to the house, and the fight was on. A short time later, Lisa began going steady with her boyfriend and I believe there was some jealously on losing their relationship.

Lisa was very headstrong, and we had tried to talk her out of going steady, but she had made up her mind and her only goal in life was to get married and have a baby. As much as we tried to talk to her about doing something else with her life before getting tied up in a relationship, she had made up her mind.

It seems that most kids will get into some kind of trouble. Sometimes it seems bad, but some small things they get in trouble for can keep them from getting into bigger trouble later when they see the consequences that came from getting into trouble. Lisa had to learn her lesson, and of course they never believe they will get caught. One evening she had decided to go to a local night club with her girlfriend. Of course they were under age, and had come up with this plan to change their drivers' licenses. They cut out their birthdates and carefully glued a new date in to make them over 21 to get into the club. They were able to get in and boy, I am sure they felt smug about their deed, but after they were there for a while a policeman walked in and began checking drivers' licenses. Of course they got caught when he began examining their cards closely. They were arrested and had to go to court.

This was a great lesson. I took her early so she could sit through all the other people that were arrested and see what happened to them. I could see the fright on her face as she waited for her turn, because lots of the kids ahead of her had done worse things and were going to jail. She was nervous at what was going to happen to her, but it was a valuable lesson, and scared her and I believe kept her from getting into any other trouble. This was very scary and humiliating for me and also for her to sit in a courtroom and await her sentence, but I stayed by her and we were both relieved when it was over. Don't bail them out. Make them suffer the consequences. They have to learn the hard way and it seems that kids don't learn any other way.

23

Our Memorable Winter Trip

Well, winter was here and we were always trying to spend some quality time with our kids and figure out how to have a good time together. It was getting harder and harder to figure out something that we could all have a good time doing, and that the kids wouldn't be bored with. We had been trying to decide what to do when we came up with the big idea to take everyone on a skiing trip. We should have had our heads examined.

A couple of them had already been skiing, and they were all wanting to learn to ski. The only problem was we didn't have any equipment, and we could not afford to buy everyone new equipment. But we had just seen an ad for the local ski swap and we figured we could get them outfitted pretty reasonable there. We had not been to one of these before. What an experience. There were probably 5,000 other people there with the same idea, it seemed like that anyway. It was a scramble. You had to crawl over and under the table to get the good bargains, but we both went and we did it, we came out victorious and we were loaded with equipment. We did not realize we had to stand in line for over an hour just to pay for these treasures, so there we stood with 7 pair of boots, 7 pair of poles, and three pair of skis, plus some ski clothes they needed. After standing in line for about ten minutes, I began to see this was really a challenge trying to juggle all this equipment. I thought, *Gee, I had seen some shopping carts in the mall where the ski swap was.* So I dumped all the equipment on the floor in front of my husband and said, "I will be back in a few minutes with a cart, so we don't have to hold all this equipment."

He looked at me like, *Oh sure, with this crowd? I am sure you will be able to get a cart in here.* But I was off, determined to come back with a cart even if it killed me, and everyone in my path. I finally spotted a cart in the mall and ran for it. I turned to forge my way back into the mob of people to find my husband buried in skis, poles and ski clothes. He was finally in sight. I don't know how I made it, he was very surprised to see me pull up with the cart, but what a relief to our already tired arms. We loaded all this into a cart for our long wait to pay for our valuables. We finally made it up to the pay station and finished our memorable day at the ski swap.

After we had purchased all this gear, we decided that we had to have some practice, so Frank took the kids out in the pasture in the snow and pulled them behind the tractor up and down hills for practice. After a short time, they finally got so one leg didn't go one way and the other the other way. They took a lot of tumbles, but they were learning to stand up on the skis and do some footwork. We all had a good time and lots of laughs. Were we ready? Well, time would tell.

So the weekend that we had scheduled for our trip finally arrived. In the camper went 7 pair of skis, poles, boots and ski clothes, and of course a large amount of food, and all seven of us piled into the pickup with the canopy. We piped heat back there from the cab, so everyone would be comfortable. We were off to the slopes. We made our way up the mountain, loaded, we got there late on Friday night, excited about the next day and our skiing adventure that was ahead of us.

Morning came and everyone was hungry. We had a good breakfast and everyone got dressed in their warm clothes to spend the day on the slopes. The kids all went full-bore all day and when evening came they were still going. We all went tubing in the evening and when everything closed down for the day, we were all exhausted, wet and hungry, of course. We headed back to our little trailer, everyone took off their wet ski clothes, which were soaked from tubing, and we hung them everywhere we could find a place to hang them to dry, in hopes they would be dry and ready to go to the slopes again the next day.

Well what an experience, if you have ever tried to eat, sleep and move around in a camp trailer with 7 people and seven sets of dripping ski clothes. The windows were steamed up and moisture was hanging everywhere. This arrangement is another one that takes lots patience and endurance on the part of parents.

The next morning we put on our sort-of dry clothes and started up the hill again. Matt was skiing fast and went over a jump, he said by accident, and broke his ski in half. Luckily, it was just before we were ready to leave, and he didn't get hurt, he just had to walk down the hill. So much for that pair of skis. They continued to ski until it was time to leave and then we all loaded up and headed down the mountain. Everyone seemed to have a great weekend. I was completely exhausted from packing, cooking and trying to keep everyone sort of dry. I sank into the seat as we traveled home and thought I should have had my head examined for even considering a trip like this.

We got home and then there was the task of unloading everything and cleaning up all the wet clothes and a dirty camper, and fixing supper. We were finally home and we finally got everything taken care of, we looked at each other and pointed up, meaning we wanted some privacy in our Blue Heaven. Off we headed up those stairs for some solitude and rest, alone at last. My husband looked at me and said "Wasn't that a relaxing wonderful weekend?" I was so tired, I was on the verge of tears.

Relaxing? Wonderful? Not my sentiments. I could think of lots of other words to describe my exhaustion and frustration of working myself to death all weekend. But I knew it was important to have fun with the children, even at the ages they were, they never seemed like they enjoyed being with us. But I know it was special to them in their lives and it helped bring us closer together.

24

SURVIVAL ON THE RANCH

Well, finally spring was here again, it was always a busy time. The irrigation water was coming on and starting to fill the canals. That precious water fed our pastures, but this also meant changing large, hand lines twice a day to get the pasture watered properly and keep it growing during the hot days of summer ahead. The wind began to blow, and suddenly we knew spring was close behind.

We purchased our calves and began watering the pasture. We were in full swing. This was a big chore and the boys always helped. They were always excited about the water coming on, and asparagus cutting coming up, but like all of us, their enthusiasm wore thin fast. Can't say that I blame them.

One morning when we were checking the calves, we noticed that some of them had sore and infected eyes. We decided to call the vet and have them examined. He came out and told us that they had a bad eye infection which must have come from one of the animals we had purchased and it would go through the entire herd of 50 calves, and they would lose their eyes if we didn't doctor them every day. Good news. He then explained to us that we would have to give them a shot in the eyes and secure a patch over their eye because it couldn't heal if light and dust got into their eyes.

So as the whole herd came down with this, we spent every evening after work getting the cattle in and locking their heads one by one in a small make-shift chute, As I tried to hold them, Frank would give them a shot in their eyes. Not an easy task, they weren't crazy about this treatment and neither was I. First one eye and then the other and then secure a patch over the worst eyes. I guess if you have ever received a shot in your eye you would understand how much they liked it and why they would not hold still for these shots that had to go between the eye layers, a delicate task. We couldn't afford to have the vet do it every day, so we took on this task, and we got pretty good at it, but it was always strenuous.

We had several of them that had to have both eyes patched because they were so bad, so we kept them in the pasture close to the house so we could keep an eye on them and they could find water and feed easier. They would wander around, feeling their way along. They looked very funny with their eyes patched.

One afternoon as we were going to check the cattle, one steer got spooked when he heard us and took off running, and he ran right through the fence. This pasture was right next to the big canal full of water, which was about 5-6 foot deep, with a bank that was about 12 feet high. He ran through the fence and across the road and sailed off the bank, dropping off into the water below. We both just stood there in terror, we ran as fast as we could, wondering what we would see when we looked to the bottom of this canal full of water. Our minds ran wild, we hated to look. Would he be dead? If not from drowning maybe from a heart attack as he went sailing through the air, not able to see where he was going, and suddenly falling into the cold water below. It must have been a terrible sensation. This was before bungee jumping came into being, but that is what I could relate it to, but there was nothing attached to bounce you back from the cold water.

We finally reached the edge of the bank and looked down and there he was swimming as fast as he could against the current. We thought, *Well, there goes $400.00 down the stream.* The current seemed to move him along fast. He was drifting towards the bridge where the road crossed over the canal, there was a small sand bar there which he caught his feet on and was able to get a foothold there. Maybe if we could get to him to help him we could save this animal, so we ran to the barn and got a couple of ropes, not sure what we were going to do for him or with them yet, but we scrambled down the side of the steep bank toward the rushing water. We got close enough to put a rope around the backside and one over his head. He was so exhausted he didn't fight us much. Now we had a rope on him, now what? How would we pull him up that steep bank and out of the water, let alone get him home.

As we were discussing a plan, a neighbor drove up in her pickup truck. She asked us if she could help, a light bulb went on and we decided maybe she could pull onto the ditch road and then we could hook the rope, which was already connected to the steer, to the bumper of the pickup and pull the steer up the ditch-bank and let him rest and then pull him home. Maybe it would work, what were our other options? So we hooked the ropes on the pickup bumper and she began slowly pulling the steer up the steep bank, as we guided the ropes to keep them secure on the steer. We had to be careful not to let them get too tight and yet stay where they needed to be to get this job done.

Slowly he began to move up the ditch-bank, we had to let him rest every few minutes, he was very weak. Finally he was at the top and we began leading this poor, blind steer up the road and into the familiar pasture he had left so abruptly. Realizing what a miracle this had all been and that it was unbelievable that we had saved this steer, after thinking what he had gone through, all we could do was say, "Praise the Lord!" and thank Him for this blessing.

I still don't know how this steer ever survived. I hope no one tried to eat him. He was probably really tough or water logged for awhile. We were finally able to take his eye patches off and his eyes were well. You would never know what he had been through, and this was a season we will never forget. After this year we decided to just rent our pasture out to other people instead of buying our own cattle. We had enough of animals to last us quite awhile, and we had saved almost all of the steers eyes. All except for just one steer had clear eyes when we shipped the cattle off to the sale in the fall, all in great shape. We gave a big sigh of relief, and were able to make our land payment one more year. Boy, did we earn that money.

25

A SPECIAL VISITOR

In the middle of raising four teenagers, we got a call from Frank's first wife. He had two other children with his first wife that she had been raising. She had kept the two younger children and he had taken the two older children. The man she had married was very jealous and would not allow Frank to have any contact with these children. This grieved his spirit every day, because he could not have a relationship with his children. We talked a lot about a solution, but without their help it was impossible.

We decided that we would at least write them once in awhile, and hoped our letters would get through, so they would at least know something about their father. It was really hard for Frank, who had agreed to let them adopt these two children after the divorce so the four children did not have to be sent back and forth. He did what he thought was best for everyone concerned, hoping they would all have a settled life. He did not want to cause a lot of trouble for his first wife or the children by forcing his way into seeing them. He knew it would only make it harder on the whole family.

By this time, he had been able to forgive his first wife, only by God's loving forgiveness is this possible for anyone. Matthew 6:14, 15, says "For if you do not forgive men their trespasses, neither will your father forgive your trespasses."

Forgiveness is so important to a happy life. So here she was on the telephone explaining that his 16-year-old son was having a hard time and was not getting along with his stepfather. His stepfather was very sick at the time, which I am sure did not help the situation. She asked if we could take Frank's son for awhile.

Well we talked about it and knew what we needed to do, but it was hard because I had never even met this child, and Frank had not seen him for years. But we wanted to help them, so we called her back and agreed to meet them halfway with all his things. Sixteen is a hard age for anyone and I am sure that was just as hard for him going to a strange home with a strange father he didn't know and a stepmother, and a whole family he did not know.

Well we picked him up. He was very quiet and I could tell there was a lot of resentment against his father, probably for not being in his life. He did not understand why this had happened. Neither parent had ever talked to him about what had happened, so it was very confusing. It must have been very frightening.

So here was another personality to deal with, one neither of us knew anything about, but we felt this was an important time in Frank's life and John's life and we were hoping we could develop some kind of a relationship with him. He desperately needed a father, and he was a good boy and tried hard to fit in, but none of us were able to pierce the shell he had built around himself.

We enrolled him in school and he loved sports so he started playing baseball, which he loved. Then, as he just got going, he broke his finger in practice and could not play anymore. That was very frustrating for him. He was close to Cindy's age so they were thrown together, doing things together most of the time, and he was assigned the job of keeping track of her if we went somewhere. She was always trying to ditch him, she was embarrassed that her brother was with her. He did a pretty good job of keeping track of her most of the time, which I am sure was not a fun job, but he tried. Our relationship with him was so limited because we did not have much of a basis to build on and he was not ready to make it work, no matter how hard we tried.

After the school year was over, his stepfather died and he decided to go back and live with his mother, which was understandable. So we packed him up and took him home, feeling somewhat a feeling of failure, but thankful that we had made some contact with John and he knew we cared. All we could hope for was a relationship in the future. Frank loved him so much, it was hard.

Contact became quite limited again until years later when he became a soldier in the Army. John was sent over to Arabia during Desert Storm. He was a bright young adult willing to be placed in harm's way for his country, we were all proud of him. As we were talking about him being there, one day we decided to get him a tape player and make tapes of how we felt. Frank explained how their lives had gotten so mixed up with the tangled web of the divorce and why Frank had stayed out of his life to make life easier for the family. As he sat out in that desert day after day waiting and listening to the tapes and thinking, he grew up a lot in that short time, emotionally and physically.

He was finally coming home from the Gulf, he was a man, no longer a boy. We were there at the airport when he came home, hoping to start a new relationship and create some memories of our own with our son.

Frank got his first Father's Day card from him that year. He sat down and cried. What a blessing for him to finally have his son back after all these years. Our relationship has blossomed and we have all become close this has been a wonderful blessing to us!

Let's face it, it is impossible for any child to realize the full extent of a parent's love until he becomes a parent himself. We praise God that there has been a healing and a forgiveness. We both love him and look forward to our times together, and we are very happy that our families can become one again through all the hurts and are so happy to find a relationship with this son. You hope after all these years of being separated from each other, that the love was still there, just buried under years of frustrations.

26

ANOTHER EXPLOSION

I was having a lot of nerve problems again, I don't know why. My hardest burden was my son, Dale, he was so much like living with my ex-husband I could not handle it. I would get so upset when he would come home and start the confusion. It was very hard on me and everyone else in the household. I knew I loved him, but I didn't like his personality. This upset me daily and I felt a lot of guilt because of my resentment to his personality, which it seemed he could not control. The sad part in all of this was he did not want to be like his dad, he hated him, but his personality was so much like his.

Frank kept on loving him even when he was unlovable and when I couldn't stand to be around him anymore. Frank had so much love to give and spent lots of time each summer teaching him his plumbing trade. He took more abuse than any man should have ever had to from that boy. But he kept trying and kept loving him, I would have killed him for sure working with him everyday with his disposition. I am so thankful for this loving man. Because of him has my son grown up and turned into a wonderful man, only unconditional love and understanding can change such a hard personality. I thank God he is finally able to tell Frank what a difference he made in his life. You hope you will see the day when your children appreciate what you did for them. It has finally arrived, praise God.

Because of the abuse my son endured from his father, he didn't allow anyone to get close to him. We tried counseling several times, but he refused to go. Life was so unbearable for everyone because of Dale's explosive personality that we had to make another decision to have some peace for us and our family. He was skipping school, which he hated by now, and we were trying to find an alternative to high school. Part of the problem was he was so behind from his surgeries on his hip that he couldn't catch up and didn't want to. We did some checking with the schools and found out that he could go to a local university under a new program and get his GED, so he would at least have that. We soon made the arrangements and he left for the program at a nearby university. He was delighted to go so he would not have to face school anymore.

This was a relief for the whole family. We all needed a break, and perhaps it would help him grow up. Plus, we all needed some peaceful existence for awhile. Most of all, we were happy because he was doing something for himself and his future.

Unfortunately that didn't last for too many months, and he was back. Life was great for awhile and then we were back to the old problems. We finally knew we had to make another hard decision to protect our family. We knew from experience that you let one child act the way he wants to and you will lose the whole family, and their respect. We explained in one of our conference times to the whole family that our home was to be a haven of peace and rest for everyone, and a shelter from the stress of the outside world. And we had to explain to them that if anyone disrupted this peace, he or she would have to be dealt with, so we had to ask Dale to leave once again. He left in a fit of anger and we didn't hear from him for a month. I finally found out he had gone to his grandfather's and then on to his dad's, where I am sure it was unbearable because they were not able to get along for very long periods of time. He kept trying to find a relationship and an acceptance by his father, which kids need so bad. It seems that if they don't find this, it haunts them their whole life. They believe they are unlovable and no one can heal that deep wound.

He finally ended up working at a nearby racetrack in a town about 30 miles away from us, sleeping in a horse stall. One of his friends told me where he had seen him, so when we were in the area we stopped by to see him. He looked like a hobo and it nearly broke our hearts, but he had to work through these things himself, and unfortunately some children have to learn by the school of hard knocks.

We visited him for a while and told him we loved him, but we had to leave him there, it was a hard time in my life. I have found that there is no other way to help your children grow up. Later, he got several other jobs and he kept losing jobs, and came home to live several times in-between jobs, broke and hungry. I finally had to make a decision to tell him if he lost the next job he had just started, he could not come home again. I told him, "If you lose your job, there is no more coming home. You will have to go to the Salvation Army or somewhere else." That was a heartbreaking thing to have to tell your son, but he knew we meant it, and he never lost another job after that. He has had a good employment record.

Sometimes, no matter how painful, you have to make them grow up and take responsibility when you only want to hold them and take them in and comfort them, but that is not what is best for them or their lives. Each child is different, some you have to push out of the nest others go easily.

27

WILL IT EVER PAY OFF?

Things became more and more difficult trying to spend time with our children. They were bored with us and embarrassed by everything we did, of course this is a natural reaction with teenage children, but that does not make it any easier when you are going through it. Each time we planned an activity for all of us, we came home very frustrated. Like, why in the world do we even try? But you have to keep trying. It seems that no matter what you do they aren't happy. We always had a least 3 mad at us at one time. I would try and make suggestions about the girls' eating habits to help them, but they really resented this. You know when you are a teenager, your parents are the enemy no matter what they try to do or say.

I always wished all our kids would marry someone with children so they could be stepparents just once in their lifetime. So far, it has only happened to one of them. My oldest son, Dale, married a wonderful girl with three little boys, their ages were 6,5, & 3. Boy, he is getting and is going to get his just reward, and he has many more to come I am afraid before they are raised. At times, he calls us and asks "How did you do this or that?" This is music to our ears. They finally realize all you sacrificed for them and you finally know something, for once in your child's life.

Another important lesson I learned while raising children was to be sure that I prayed for each child before they began their day. They seemed to respond better and always had a better day. I didn't always pray for them aloud or in their presence, but many times I would pray for them upon waking in the morning or after they had left for school.

Mothers: Remember, it is so important when you send your children out in this wicked world to pray for them each day. I could always tell the days I got busy and forgot to pray for them by their disposition when they got home from school, and by the difficulty day they had. They need your prayers so desperately, all through their lives and they never get too old to pray for. God can make a difference in their lives, each day, and I feel he keeps his protection around them as they walk through the valley of death and destruction of this world, and struggle with maturing and growing up into adults. It is no an easy process for any of them to resist temptation and build happy lives. And always remember: give them your love and most of all your time.

I heard a definition of love one time, it was:

The definition of love is spelled: T-I-M-E.

Please remember the teenage years are hard, but they will grow up and finally realize that you really love them, and they will appreciate what you did for them when they start raising kids of their own. Sometimes you have to remember this to get through those rough teenage years. I always say that God gave us teenagers so that by the time they are ready to leave home, you are glad to see them go or don't feel too bad about it. At least at this time you figure it is best for everyone concerned.

My best experience was when my oldest daughter had her first baby. At last, I really got smart and she loved to hear what I had to say, and we even enjoyed each other. What a blessing, so hang in there and remember some day it will get better, if you hang in there long enough.

28

LOTS OF EXCITEMENT

Things began to heat up between Lisa and her boyfriend. They became engaged and a fall wedding was planned. The same weekend, they became engaged was also the weekend that Debbie's high-school royalty pageant was going on. She had entered the pageant for the high-school royalty, so I knew that this was going to be some weekend for excitement. We had promised Lisa and her fiancé that we would take them out to eat to celebrate their engagement. It seemed like you are always trying to make everyone's special time special. It takes lots of energy, money and patience.

Debbie's pageant was to be on Saturday and her mother and her younger sister were going to get to come to see it. I was so happy for all of them, and I had not met this younger daughter and Frank had not seen her since she was little, so it was an exciting time. It was a rare event that she would have her mother and sister come to see her and especially for something that was so special. I was happy for her because it used to break my heart when her mother would stop by and see her, and then have to drive away and leave her daughter again. I can't imagine the pain she experienced. These children would both be crying when she left and it would take them days to recover, wondering when they would see her again.

Of course, having company, especially a sister and ex-wife, put added pressure on me. With an engagement to celebrate, trying to be equally happy for each child, and fulfilling what they each needed during this special time was very hard.

We had put some money aside to take Lisa and her fiancé out to dinner like we had promised. I had also planned a nice dinner at home for Debbie and her mother and sister to share. I thought I had everyone taken care of, but as we were getting ready to leave for our engagement party, Debbie came to her father and said she had decided to take her mother and sister out to dinner, and of course needed money for this. So after all my planning, things were in a big turmoil once again, and everyone was upset and mad. We had only planned financially for our dinner and everything was ready for Debbie and her guests at home.

To say the least, I was really mad, but of course you always feel guilty, or you go through, *I should have planned things differently*. But after much talking between Frank and I in Our Blue heaven, she was told that she would have to stick to the plan and eat the dinner I had planned at home, which caused another tear-jerking scene. It had to be that way because that was how it was all planned beforehand, and I knew it was hard for Frank to disappoint his daughter, but after our discussion, we both knew it was right.

We were finally off for our engagement party in a state of frustration and guilt, even though we know we made the right decision. But in spite of the turmoil, we decided to have a nice evening in spite of it all, and it was a special evening.

The next evening was the beauty pageant to elect the queen and princess to represent our town and ride the float in the parades. This was also a great moment for Debbie. We were all so excited. It was a nice evening, and Debbie was crowned the princess. She looked so beautiful and played a trumpet solo for her talent portion of the program. She did a great job, but afterwards she found out she had left her mute in her trumpet and forgot to take it out while she played. She was so embarrassed. But I don't think many people knew the difference, she just had to blow a lot harder to get the volume out of the trumpet, but it still sounded great. We had a celebration afterwards, and everyone was so happy for her. I was so glad her mother and sister could share this time with her.

Later on in the week, we went to the meeting to find out the parents' responsibilities and what role we had to play this year. But luckily, we didn't know what was really expected of us. We spent evenings working on the float building it. It was a slow process. We would both drag home from work and have our supper and be off to build the float in a cold, old building down the road.

Well the parades were starting. They were every weekend of the summer, we didn't go every weekend. They always had chaperones that were assigned to go with them. We had bought an older motor home which worked great to go to the parades.

One particular parade we helped with, which really stands out in my mind, was an evening, lighted parade in Portland, Oregon. We worked all day on the float. In

Portland, it was hot and we were tired, but we finally got all the lights on the float working at one time, which is a big job in a lighted parade.

We had to be ready for the 10:00PM evening parade. So before the float left to join the parade, we decided that we had better look for a place to park so we could get near and watch the parade pass, and admire our work. We looked and looked for a safe place without a sign saying: TOW AWAY ZONE. After driving and driving and seeing lots of cars looking for a parking place, we finally located what we thought was a safe place to park our motorhome. We parked and walked to the parade, being very careful to remember where we had parked so we could find our motorhome after the parade was over.

We enjoyed the parade, it was a long one, but beautiful with all the lights. It was getting very late and we were exhausted. We hiked back, street by street, to be sure we were correct in finding our motorhome and our bed awaiting us and lay our tired bodies down.

As we walked and walked and searched and searched trying to remember if this was really the correct place we had left our motorhome, we could not find our motorhome. We were sure we were in the correct spot, but where was our motorhome? Nowhere to be found. Everywhere we looked, we could see tow trucks towing cars away parked in no-parking zones. It was getting very disturbing, and we wondered, *Has this happened to us?* You would think with this large crowd in town, they would be lenient to let people park and enjoy the parade for a couple of hours, but no such luck. They were making all kinds of money out of this parade, and the faithful tourists that were there to see the parade were really getting a raw deal. It was disgusting.

So in our despair, we decided we would have to find a

policeman to ask how we could find our motorhome and check to see if it had been towed away. We hiked back uptown, we were about 15 blocks from the parade route. We finally reached the main street and spotted a policeman and asked him what we should do. He suggested we call the place that towed cars and see if our motorhome had been towed away. He gave us the telephone number and went on directing traffic.

By this time it was around midnight, and we finally got through to their impound lot. We explained what our motorhome looked like and, sure enough, they had towed it there. They said, "You will have to come down to the lot, meet someone there and be let in, and of course bring $85.00 in cash."

Oh, great. So we hiked down and found our group that was dismantling the float and everyone helped us come up with the $85.00. We did not carry that much cash around so we were in a real jam.

Then we were off to redeem our motorhome and our bed, discovering it was about 20 blocks to the impound lot. With the traffic the way it was, it was easier to walk, besides everyone else was tied up with taking the float down and putting it away for the trip home. We walked and walked and began to feel very uncomfortable about the part of town we were getting into. The people that were in this neighborhood looked pretty scary. We kept walking, I said, "We will probably get killed or mugged for our $85.00 before we get there to redeem our motorhome." I was so mad I could see stars, but we finally reached the lot. It was under a railroad bridge and a dark uncomfortable place to be at that time of night.

We got up to the gate, which was locked, and we could not see anyone around so we finally decided to hike back up to the telephone and call again to see if someone would meet us at the impound lot. Someone, luckily, answered the telephone and agreed to meet us there shortly. We would try once again.

So off we hiked back to that dark place in that terrible part of town again, and sat there on the curb. This must have been one of the worst parts of town in Portland, and there we sat late at night, waiting for someone to come meet us so we could finally claim our motorhome and get out of here. I was barely coherent by this time with being tired, and so mad. Do you blame me?

They finally came and opened the gate and there sat our motorhome, what a wonderful sight. So we paid our fine and roared out of there, wanting to say lots, but mumbling all sorts of things you don't want to hear, because they would be censored. I looked at Frank and said, "Let's get out of this terrible town as fast as we can, I am not spending another minute more than I have to here."

So we drove out of town a little while and stopped in a grocery store parking lot absolutely exhausted and frustrated from our experience. We finally dropped into bed, at least knowing that we would not be towed away in our sleep, like we could have been if we had stayed in Portland. This was not a good experience for us, not exactly the highlight of our year on the float team.

It was a great year for Debbie, she had a great time, and got lots of enjoyment out of it. They all made lots of friends and learned a lot. I am sure it was a year she will never forget.

29

OUR FIRST WEDDING

Well, we were going through summer and planning the wedding for our oldest daughter, Lisa, which she was planning for the fall. It was a busy summer. Of course in her eyes, money was no object. Kids think it grows on trees anyway. We decided after a few weeks of hearing the plans, something had to be done about the things she was planning and the costs that were beginning to add up. We decided we needed one of our famous summit meetings, of course in our Blue Heaven, so we sat down and figured out what we could afford to spend on this wedding and since she was working, she could pay the rest of whatever she wanted to spend on this wedding. We do not believe in going into debt for the things our kids want because we have to work hard for our money.

So we sat her down and told her the amount of money we were going to contribute to this cause, and the rest was hers to do, and she could do whatever she wanted. We always stressed to our children, "You can have anything you want in life, you just have to work for it."

Boy, things changed after that. When the realization of what everything costs set in with her, it was an eye-opener for her. We finally found a more reasonable dress, not like the one she had planned on earlier before the budget crash. She had a hard time with the other decisions, of course she didn't like anything I suggested or picked out, so we were not in accord on too many things. I guess this is a normal complaint. She made a lot of changes and did without a few things, which didn't affect the wedding any, and no one knew the difference.

Finally, the day was fast approaching. I hoped we were ready. As a mother of a bride, it is always scary, especially planning your first wedding. You worry too much, and everything always seems to go OK. Only you and the bride know if it doesn't go accordingly.

When you are young, time isn't important, and I always say you are making the most important decisions of your life, for a career and a spouse, and you have no idea of what you want in either matter and have no experience behind you to make the proper decision.

I can't figure how we could ever change this fact of life. It doesn't seem right, of course there are lots of things in life that don't seem right. After our talk, she was still determined to get married and have a baby. She would never talk of any kind of career plans, so we gave up and proceeded with our wedding plans.

The evening came for the rehearsal and it went great. we had a nice dinner party for the wedding party, and all anticipating the coming day.

Then, the morning was here and we all were going to get our hair fixed before the wedding. This also included our youngest daughter, Cindy, who was to be a candle lighter with the groom's sister in the wedding. I dropped her off to get her hair fixed and I went on to do some other errands I needed to get done and get my hair fixed. She was always the kind of child who wanted to be different and didn't care what other people thought about her decision. I should have not let her go to the beauty shop without me, but I had lots to do and figured, *What could go wrong at the beauty shop?*

When I arrived to pick her up, she had this new haircut she was so proud of. I took one look at her and almost got sick. She had them shave the back of her head halfway up and then this shaved line went all the way from the back to the front. Of course being a candle lighter in the wedding, the back of her head would show more than anything else. That was what most people would see the most of.

I headed towards home sick, not knowing what to do. As I came through the door, the bride took one look and began to cry. My mother looked at it and was really mad. I had a young girl who was so proud of her new haircut and couldn't understand why we didn't all love it too. What were we going to do, just hours before the wedding. If only I had time to get my hands on that beauty operator. It was one of her young friends, and she had told him she wanted something different that would wow everyone. I am sure it would have, in this very conservative church wedding.

We had to come up with some idea to cover that head. The only answer was a hat, which meant we had to have two matching hats for both girls. We started calling everywhere trying to find two hats and luckily we located two hats. I ran down and bought them and after adding a few flowers to the hats, they looked like they belonged in the wedding.

Thank goodness she would not embarrass the whole family and the new in-laws. You would think *once* things would just go smoothly.

We luckily survived this and the wedding and everything else went smoothly, and it was a beautiful wedding. The couple were off on their honeymoon and were going to make their home in a city about 3-hours drive from where we were living. He was starting a new job and we felt the distance would be good for them, and they would have to make it on their own without interference from parents. They were on their own...one down, four to go...

Since then, I have learned that they are never on their own. There is always something happening in their lives. You do a lot of praying and your thoughts are never very far from them. It is hard seeing your children pick their mates, and you wish you could pick them for them. You are sure you would make good choices, but we have learned to love all our sons-in-law and daughters-in-law, so I guess they really don't need our help after all.

30

OUR CADET

The next year was also a busy year. Matt was graduating from high school and had received an appointment to West Point, the army academy. He had worked very hard since he started high school to get this appointment. You have to start in your sophomore year and take certain courses, and get excellent grades and participate in some sports. You have to have a well-rounded education and excel in everything. We felt all our fighting and frustrations with him seemed finally right, when we reached this point.

When he received this acceptance, we were so glad that he had finally adjusted to society and become socially active. It would help him with this large future he was taking on. You always hope you are doing the right thing, and sometimes through the struggles you really wonder if it is worth it. But it is. Remember, with your children, some of the really hard things are the best things you can do for them.

He was off to get his physical and then came graduation from High school, and right after that he would leave for New York and West Point, a long way from home.

He was only 17 years old. He was very young compared to a lot of the boys and he was going so far from home, and to a place where they showed no one any mercy.

This is a very hard school. It has very strict discipline and a hard physical routine for these young boys, but great training. They are so hard on these young boys, it breaks your heart, when you hear some of what goes on. One-fourth of the class dropped out by Christmas, because they could not take it anymore. They can't have any personal things, radios, and they have no life for the first year. They just study and build their minds and bodies. Matt held in there, he knew what he wanted.

I am sure there were lots of times he wanted to give up, but he didn't. It was what he had wanted to do for a long time. He had a wonderful mind and I think what kept him going was he just put himself into his books and studies, and tried to block all the other unpleasant things out that were going on around him. He had to stick it out for 4 years, which is a long time.

I asked a general at West Point when we were there for graduation, "Why are they so mean to these poor boys so far away from home?"

The general answered, "If they can't take it, we don't want them. They have to be tough and well trained. They are our future leaders and they have to be mentally controlled at all times to make life-threatening decisions without a lot of thinking. It has to become natural and they have to be strong in every aspect of their lives."

I gulped. I guess that is true, but it is still hard from a mother's standpoint. They really make men of these boys, and develop their minds and bodies to be the utmost specimens.

Matt made a lot of lifetime friends there. They all shared the good and the bad together, but no one can understand, I am sure, unless you have been there and lived it, how tremendously hard it is.

Christmas was coming and Matt would get his first leave and be able to come home, and have a break which I am sure he desperately needed and was really looking forward to.

31

OUR CADET COMES HOME

Christmas was here and Matt finally came home. You can't image what a change. We had sent a boy and he came home a man, in just a few months, the change was unbelievable. He had learned to take a bath without being told, and change his socks, and even wear matching ones. All through high school he had a bad habit of taking two socks out of the sock box that didn't match. It would make Dale so mad because then he wouldn't have any matching socks either. He was so absent-minded you would never believe he had such a high IQ, and could accomplish so much in his life. I don't know how many push-ups and potatoes he had to peel to learn these lessons, but he had learned them well.

He got to stay home for a week and he was busy seeing all his friends. He looked so grown up in his dress uniform, which he was required to wear most of the time he was home. We were very proud of him and his accomplishments. He was doing very well in his studies, but was working hard to accomplish what the demands of this school were. It is wonderful to finally see your children grow up and become fine young people with a purpose in life.

The academy is so strict on everything that he told us even when they are eating they are regimented. He told us they all have to sit at attention, a certain way, and all have to pick up their forks and put them down while chewing their food. If one cadet makes a mistake, they are all punished and don't get to finish their meal, because they all have to sit at attention for their punishment and most of the time their meal time is up, and they haven't finished. It still doesn't seem right to me, but who am I? Only a concerned mother.

He stayed for his week and then he had to go back, I could see that he was not excited about it, but he did what he had to do and went back to face the rest of the year.

He only had a short vacation in the summer, so we did not get to see much of him in those four years, but we sent care packages and time seemed to pass fast for us. I am sure a lot slower for the cadets.

After the first year, they were able to have more privileges and could write and have a little life. But Matt was never much for writing. We all usually all got a computer letter once a year, but he would call sometimes in-between. They were kept very busy and had little time for themselves. We were very proud of his accomplishments at West Point and I know he was a fine soldier.

When we went there for his graduation, we were very proud. It was a little confusing because there was his mother and grandmother and a stepmother. Sometimes the situation was uncomfortable, but you have to remember the children and keep telling yourself you are doing this for them, not for yourself. You have to be on guard and not let things upset you when you are in this type of situation with ex-spouses and families. It usually takes a lot of talking to yourself to get through it. Graduation was an exciting time for everyone and he received many honors for graduating the top of his class, including a three-year scholarship to Stanford University to complete his education. He had made many friends and we were all amazed at these fine young men and their accomplishments.

32

THE NEST IS EMPTYING OUT

Debbie was busy planning on going to college. I think she was caught up in it because her friends were going and she did not know what she wanted to take for sure. She had been working at a flower shop through high school and saved some for college.

We were talking about college and we did not have any extra money for college. We talked and talked to her about going to just a year school for a trade or something that did not require a four-year college, and she could get a job sooner, and wouldn't have to finish four years to be able to do anything. But she had made up her mind, and I know school away from home sounded so exciting. Things are really different when you actually get there and have to live college life.

We have seen so many of our friends send their kids off to college and the kids have no idea what they want to take, and the kids literally break their folks because they are not contributing, they don't take college seriously. We decided that she would have to spend her own money and apply for loans if she wanted to go. You really feel cruel, but she did get some school loans and got ready to start her first year.

Fall came soon. She loaded up the pickup and was ready to move to college. We drove her there, three hours away, and finally got the pickup unloaded. Of course everything had to go upstairs. Her roommate seemed to be a nice girl, that was a relief.

When we arrived home, we looked around and said, "Boy, it is getting quiet in our home and things are changing fast. Another one left the nest."

The year passed and she finished her first year. At that point, she decided college was not for her so she did not go back. But it was a valuable life experience and she made many friends, and learned a lot about life and living.

33

ANOTHER NEW RELATIONSHIP

The Lord provided another beautiful opportunity to connect with Frank's youngest daughter. He had never even gotten to hold this girl as a baby, and missed out on her development and it gnawed at his heart. We received a call from Martha one evening and she let us know she was going to perform with a singing church group in a nearby church. This was very exciting that she would want us to be there. She was searching for some answers to, and with her stepfather gone, she wanted to find out about her real father.

Frank had very little contact with her from the time her stepfather had adopted her, which had broken his heart. We finally were able to talk to her about this just recently and she told us of all her mixed feelings during this first encounter. It is so sad how kids get hurt no matter how you try to do the best for them.

We listened to them sing and then after we were able to spend some time together. She was now 16 and it was the first time Frank got to hold her and put his arms around her. It was a very moving time for everyone. I am sure there were lots of mixed feelings of resentment. Later on in our talks, she told us this was really a hard time in her life as she tried to figure out what had happened and why this man was coming into her life now. Where had he been and who was he to just step in after so many years and love her? She never was told or understood the situation that caused the divorce and wasn't told why her father did not come to see her or contact her, and it was a very hurtful part of her life.

Finally, she had to leave with her group. It had been a great time, full of lots of emotions and wondering when we would see each other again. She later went to the Philippines for a year during high school, so we did not get to develop a relationship with her until later in her life. When she was married, we began to develop a relationship and she began to be able to forgive and deal with this as an adult.

Since her wedding, which we attended, we have become very close and we love her and her husband, and have begun talking about all these feelings, trying to receive healing, and understand this tangled web of all our lives. She has the Lord in her life, and that has helped with the forgiveness and healing. We are grateful for that. It is so special to have a relationship with her now. We really enjoy her and her husband's company and love. It means the world to Frank and I love her, too. Our relationship is becoming deep, and I guess it is never too late. We are so thankful that we have reached that level with his two younger children of forgiveness and acceptance that we all need so badly. After the years of torture and not being able to be part of their lives and wondering and worrying about them and praying for their happiness, it is so good to be part of their lives. Praise God for forgiveness and healing for all of us. I know there are many in this world that need it so desperately. I'm glad we have all found it.

34

OUR FIRST GRANDCHILD

Our daughter, Lisa, called us and told us that she was expecting her first baby. We were so happy for them. We were ready to be grandparents, but we weren't sure our kids were ready. Time seemed to go by quickly and she wanted me to be with her when she went to the hospital. I had explained to her that this was a special time for her and her husband, and I wanted them to share this special moment together. I told her I would be there right after the delivery. I did not want to interfere with this special time.

I have always tried not to be a mother-in-law that is always there in the middle of things. They called me and told me she had gone to the hospital, so I began packing to go help her for a few days.

What an exciting time. I drove those three hours with much anticipation. When I arrived there, I found out she had already had a beautiful little boy and she would be coming home the next day, and I would be there to help her.

Talk about a change in a girl. Here was my little headstrong child that never listened to anything I ever said, finally wanting my advice, and even listening to it. I knew something after all the years of being so dumb.

We brought the baby home and had such a great time taking care of him and sharing, and developing a whole new friendship we had never had before in our lives together. We bathed him and shared many special moments. I could see she was a good mother, and his dad loved him so much. It was wonderful to see your children grow up and have their own children. It makes all those years of struggle worthwhile after all.

I stayed for a few days and then returned home, leaving that little bundle of joy with them to raise and nurture. Praying that he would grow up to be a fine young man, and turning him over to the Lord for safe keeping. Sharing this with your daughter is really one of life's great moments, and an unforgettable experience that no mother should miss.

35

MAJOR CHANGES IN OUR LIVES

We were having a struggle financially because the community we lived in was primarily agriculture and farming and these were both at an all-time low. We had to make a decision on what we were going to do while we still had some money to make a move and start making a living somewhere else.

We prayed about where we were to go and had no idea of where to start, somewhere there were jobs, we knew that. A week later, we received a call from a builder who we had worked for earlier in the year who had moved to the city because of our economy. As Frank began to talk to him about what he was doing in the city, he said, "By the way, I called to ask you if you would come work for me in the city." He had just started building there and needed a plumber to help him with his job. We felt that was our answer on what we were supposed to do.

We always believed you have to put feet to your prayers, and when God opens up a door, you have to move through. That is our part of the plan. So we loaded up our motorhome and went to look things over.

After a few days in the city, we had made our decision to move there. What did we have to lose? At least there were jobs there. I had never lived in a city and Frank had only lived in a city for a few years previous to our marriage, but it looked so exciting, and people had money and positive attitudes about their lives, as compared to the agriculture community we were in where everyone was always on the verge of losing their crops and farms. When there was a water shortage or a frost to kill the crops, things were pretty bleak, and no one spent any money they didn't have to.

We had wonderful neighbors. Our family doctor, who was one of our neighbors, I can't tell you how many times he came to our rescue when one of the kids had been hurt. He sewed them up when they ran into the fence on their motorcycle, and was a dear friend too and on several occasions we had fixed his plumbing when he called us. We would miss all these wonderful neighbors, but this economy was really dragging us down, emotionally and financially. We had to do this to support ourselves and go on with our lives.

We made our decision to move to the city, but just moving there with no jobs. We did not know anyone except this one builder. It was quite a challenge.

There were so few rentals. We tried and tried on several trips to find a home to rent. Of course coming from the farm, we had a van, car, pickup and boat, and everything we looked at had a garage and one parking place behind the garage. What were we going to do? There must be a place somewhere in this large city for us. We knew God had something in store for us after making it clear that this was where we were to be, so we had to keep searching. Several times we came back home discouraged, not knowing what to do next.

Later that week, we got a call from a friend of ours, a local farmer, and after telling him our plan we found out he had an aunt in the city who had a home. She had been hit in a crosswalk and was in a nursing home which could be quite a while. He said he would get in touch with her about her empty home. He called her and she was happy to rent her home. At this point, we were not fussy, we just needed a room and a roof over our heads. So here in the middle of this big city, God found us a place on one acre, with plenty of parking only 10 blocks from downtown for (get ready for this) $200.00 a month.

We were excited and amazed, but wondered what we would get for $200.00. So off we went again, wondering what new adventure was in store for us now. Everything else we had looked at had been at least $700.00 and up, so we knew something had to be different about this place we were about to live in. But we were ready to take anything.

Good thing our minds were in this state. It was a real gem. The blackberry bushes had grown over the house and you could hardly see it. You could not see out of the windows because of the bushes running up the side of the house. As we went in we noticed that the ceiling had been leaking and mold was running up the walls everywhere from the moisture because the house had been closed up for quite awhile. But we looked at each other and decided that God had provided it for us and we would fix it up. We were good at that and we had lots of time to do some repairs. We could make it a comfortable home and be thankful no matter what.

We began our supreme challenge with scrubbing all the mold off the walls, painting the inside and chopping weeds and blackberries until we couldn't go any longer. In the bedroom, the ceiling had fallen in from the roof leaking so badly, so we decided we needed to do something about the roof before the rains started, before we did much more inside.

We decided for $200.00 a month, and no income yet, it was just what we needed to supply our needs, and a little work would make it cozy, fresh and clean. Of course it started raining before we got the room fixed, and we had buckets sitting everywhere and had to sleep on the hide-a-bed in the living room because that was the only spot that didn't leak.

This home also had a basement so we fixed Cindy a room down there which would be dry. When the rain slowed down, we started fixing the flat roof.

What a job.

There were layers and layers of old roofing so we had to cut it in squares and shovel it off, and clear some space for a new roof. Flat roofs are really hard to keep from leaking, but we finally got it sealed up and the ceiling fixed inside. It was even becoming cozy.

Cindy was enrolled in school. This was quite a change for her from a small, country community. We all had lots of changes to deal with, but we knew this was our new adventure and we were supposed to be there. We really had to rely on God for every avenue in our lives, and we soon discovered a valuable lesson. That when you totally rely on God, you can see his hand in everything and how he blesses you everyday.

Frank began making contacts with several general contractors, hoping to find some more work, and stopping to leave a resume with them, and taking some time to talk to them. He finally found a plumbing contractor that needed some extra help, so he worked for him part time until his own contracting would began.

I started selling real estate, which was very challenging since I had never lived in a city before. I was always lost and had never read a map so that was a difficult task, but I kept trying, with a maximum of frustration.

Cindy was doing pretty well, except she was ashamed of our home and would not tell anyone where she lived. When she mowed the lawn out front, whenever she would hear a car coming down the road in front where she was mowing, she would run for the house so no one would see her in the yard and recognize her and know where she lived. She finally found some friends, which was a relief, and began to find out they didn't care where she lived. By the time she was able to bring the kids home, we had the house in pretty good shape. Of course it did not compare with the big homes some of her friends had, but to lots of kids that was really not important.

We were really being blessed and the curtains in the living room were so bad. I wanted to replace them, but money was tight and we would have to make these do, but God knows our needs. One day as I was driving down a street near our home, I saw a yard sale. I decided to stop and as I looked there were two pair of drapes, exactly the size and color we needed for our home. They were very cheap. I couldn't believe it, I kept checking the sizes. I was so excited as I drove off with my blessing headed towards home to show the family how good God was. They fit perfectly and we were so blessed, and special things like this do so much for your state of mind.

The only thing left that we needed to finish this home and make it cozy was carpet. We had old, cold, wood floors, and there had been a lot of water on them from the leaking roof, so they weren't too nice looking. But God knew and a few weeks later Frank and I went to get him some business cards printed. As we got out of the car to go into the print shop, we noticed a fancy furniture store right in front of us. They were remodeling and I could see they were re-carpeting their store. Then I saw them throwing out all the carpet in the street right in front of us.

I went in and said, "What are you going to do with that old carpeting?"

They said, "Nothing. Do you want it?"

So we loaded up all this great carpet and it carpeted our whole house and really made a difference. What a blessing that carpet was, and it was even the color we had wanted. I said to Frank, "Can you believe it.?"

And he said, "Yes, can't you?"

Frank's business began growing. First, one contractor let him do one job and try him out, and soon they were referring him to other contractors. He felt so good to be earning money again and getting our lives back on track. We met a lot of nice people even in the city. We were thankful that they gave us a chance and helped us get started. It was really a change in every way for us, and we began enjoying the excitement of the city.

I was still trying to sell real estate, but it was such a stressful job. I did not know how long I could it. I was really struggling with trying to find my way and read maps, and I was always lost. I finally gave up and went to work to have a steady income. We had hoped to build our own home after we got our home in the country sold. We could see there was no way we could afford a home in the city if we had to buy one, so we figured our only option would be to build one. So I figured a steady income would help us if we needed money to build a home and get any kind of financing.

36

THE MIDNIGHT RIDE

Cindy seemed to be doing pretty good, she had made new friends and had settled down some.

One evening, after we had all gone to bed early, we were sleeping sound when we heard the telephone ring. It was the local police, which woke us up right away, the policeman said, "Do you have a yellow Toyota car?"

My husband said, "Yes," reluctantly.

The next question was, "Do you have a daughter named Cindy?" This was beginning to sound suspicious.

He said, "Yes," again, wondering in his sleepy state what was going on. The officer began to tell him he had just stopped a yellow car with a girl named Cindy driving, and when he checked the registration the car was registered to Francis Garceau, so he called us.

He said she had been out driving with her friends riding in the car with her. A few blocks from our house they were going so slow that the police officer became suspicious of them and stopped them. My husband said, "Just a minute. I will go check. I am sure our Cindy is in her bed."

He jumped up and ran downstairs to check. He peaked in the bedroom with apprehension and noticed the bed looked like she was there in the bed. But the old trick was played on us of stuffing the bed to look like she was still there. He ran to the garage in the basement next to her bedroom and his heart leaped. The car was gone and so was she.

He came running upstairs with a look of terror on his face. I knew immediately what the policeman had said was true. He got back on the telephone gulping, "Well, I guess that is my daughter and my car. We will be right up to get her."

By that time, I was very upset, but we jumped out of bed sick to our stomachs and got dressed and headed up to our little yellow car, full of kids.

There sat the car along the road with a big, delightful, black policeman standing alongside the car, with three crying girls sitting in the car.

Cindy had apparently been out cruising and she had picked up her friends to join her for her ride. They were having lots of fun, but was unsure of driving. She was only 13 and had no driving experience at this point except sitting on Frank's lap, driving around the pasture on the farm, which was a far cry from taking a car out in the city. So she was driving very unsure of herself. Of course it was 3:00 in the morning and there weren't very many people out on the roads. This car full of kids looked suspicious to the police officer, and luckily he stopped them before they really got into lots of trouble.

There they sat as we walked up to the car, crying and

the big policeman was standing there beside the car, he reached out his hand and said, "Hi, my name is Hershey." I almost laughed. It was one of those times when you don't know whether to laugh or cry, but his name struck a funny bone somewhere, it fit him so completely. I am sure the girls were scared to death, as large as he was and as scared as they were of the trouble they would be in now, being discovered in their "midnight drive."

We told the girls to get out of the car, and they were still crying, asking us not to tell their parents. The officer had given them quite a talking to and he insisted on taking the other girls home to their parents, which was quite all right with us, since I did not want to face their parents at this point. So we took our bundle of joy home and brought the car home. Luckily, he never gave her a ticket or she would not have been able to get her driver's license for quite awhile.

After a lot of talking, we were confident that she had learned her lesson, without too serious of consequences, and luckily no one was hurt. But many years later we learned this had not been her first midnight ride. She had been doing this for quite awhile before she was caught. She would push the car out the driveway so we could not hear the car start and then jump in and coast down the hill and start the car and be off to get her friends for their city cruise.

We decided to ground her for awhile. I think this was lesson #10 for her. It might have been #312, I am not sure, but there were many more to come in her life. She did not learn the easy way, and like most teenagers thought she would never get caught, and did. Anyway, she never took the car again until after she got her license, and got permission.

37

ANOTHER ADVENTURE

We finally sold our home in the country, so we began looking for a place to build, which was not easy in the city. There weren't many lots available. We knew we would have to build and use the money from the sale of our other home in order to afford a home in the city. So as we were driving around we were always looking for lots, but they were always so expensive.

One day as I was driving around from work, I spotted a sign that just went up about two blocks from where we lived. It was a treed lot. I ran down and found out the information on it and hurried up and made an offer on it. I knew with the shortage of lots we had to act fast to secure this lot so close in.

So our lot was purchased and we began making plans to build a home and finally get a place of our own again. We finalized our plans for our new home and began getting permits. After that was accomplished, we began clearing our lot for our new home.

This was a big project with both of us working full time. We were busy building every evening until 11:00 or 12:00, and every weekend. You have to keep telling yourself nothing worthwhile is easy, anyway that had always been our philosophy throughout our married lives, not sure we have convinced ourselves yet though.

We finally got the home closed in and it was taking shape and looking like a home, we were about four months away from getting close to moving in. Of course it was far from finished, but we figured we could move in and finish it. The telephone rang one evening and it was the lady we were renting from and she said, "I want my house back in a week." She had been living in an apartment close to her doctor, recovering from her injuries and she felt she was well enough to move back into her home.

Frank said, "In a week? That's impossible. I will try and be out in a month. That's the best I can do, the way rentals are." When he got off the telephone we discussed what we would do. He called her back, but there was no reasoning with her about letting us stay in the house until our house was finished. After all the fixing we had done to the house, and our lot was so close it had been an ideal situation and now we had to find another place to live for a short period of time, which would make it even harder to rent something. But we kept our faith and knew we could depend on God and He was still there and faithful and would be looking out for us.

We looked for a solid week, and no one wanted to rent to us because we would not be staying very long, most people wanted a year's lease. Well, I guess we would have to turn this one over to God and wait for another miracle.

We were finally down to only one more week until we

had to move. We went to church that Sunday trying not to be discouraged, and trying very hard to trust God for our answer of where we were going to live. We were so discouraged with house hunting. This was not an easy task.

We went to a large church and didn't know very many people to ask for help. After we left church that Sunday, we stopped by a small restaurant nearby for lunch. At lunch, we met this lovely couple and began visiting with them. They mentioned they had seen us in church and we were excited to meet someone from the church. We visited quite awhile. As we visited, we found out they were in the rental business and had quite a few rentals. So we shared our dilemma with them, but they didn't have any vacancies at this point. After a while he said, "I have a house I had for an office for quite a while, and I have just retired from my business. So if you help me clean it out of my office things, I will rent it to you reasonably."

Oh boy, just what we wanted, another house to fix up. But, as usual, how choosy can you be? It turned out to be a nice house We helped them move all their things out and did a little painting and moved in. God is always faithful. This was a nice house we moved in and it was great for Cindy because she felt more comfortable about bringing her friends there, which was good for her.

We finally got our home closed in and we had one bathroom finished and linoleum in the kitchen and eating area, and one interior door on the bathroom. We decided it was time to stop paying rent and move in. So in we moved and I scrubbed the bare floors and we borrowed a little combination stove, sink and refrigerator from our friend we had been renting from so we would have some form of a kitchen to set up housekeeping in our new home. Well, sort of...

We were happy. We only had one small problem. We were out of money. Not so small a problem, we decided, after we thought about it.

We had tried to make our money stretch as far as we could. We had done remarkably well to get what we did finished, but as you know money goes fast and everything costs more than you planned. If you have ever built a home, you would understand. So our only solution was we would have to go to the bank and get a loan to finish our home.

Building in the city is no easy task, especially for two hicks from the sticks. We had the fire engine there twice and were almost arrested because we burned some of our brush we cleared. We had to continually wash the street, because you can not get any dirt on the city streets there or they would hire a sweeper to clean it and charge it to us. And mine permit fees were some of the strangest we ever experienced, which had not helped our budget. We had learned a lot about building in the city, which helped us later down the road on other projects we did. It was a real learning experience for us.

So off to the bank we went confidently. Well, if you have ever been self employed, new to a city, starting a new business, or have built your own house or any one of these things you will realize what we were up against with bankers. They listen a few minutes, get a red neck and avoid you like the plague. Of course every red flag goes up when you start talking to them about what you have done, and they know they have to try and explain all this to a superior.

They said, "You want what?" They get an instant picture in their minds of a do-it-yourself home builder. Of course they envision this house pieced together, on the verge of collapse, which scares them to death. Of course no one knew our track record and what we were capable of doing, which didn't help. They hate dealing with owner/builders because lots of people don't understand what it takes to build a home.

We talked and talked to bankers. We couldn't even get one to come look at what we had already finished. Then one day, I was talking to some of my real estate friends and they told me that my old real estate broker who hired me when I first came to the city had since left for another job working for a loan company in the city. I hoped maybe he would work with us and give us a personal reference. We had also done some construction work for him, so he was a little familiar with our talents, and we had become friends during the time I worked for him. Maybe there was a chance for us to get a loan through him. So off we went to see him to tell him our problems and hope he could help us. We put in our application and everyday they wanted more information, and we would have to take in more figures for them to look at to prove ourselves. This went on for almost a month, but I kept hanging in there. My husband who had not dealt with bankers had given up by this time and he said, "They want everything including my short size. I guess I will put them in the copy machine and send them a copy of the size. Maybe that will satisfy them."

We finally got the OK, I am sure with a lot of vouching for us by my past employer, bless him. We were so excited. We could finally finish our home and have a kitchen and some flooring and another bathroom upstairs. We went in that fateful day and signed the final papers. We had made a list of the things we needed to purchase with the money we would need to draw that day to get our project completed. We signed the papers and then presented our information on our draw to finish our projects to the loan officer. He looked at us strangely and said, "Oh you don't get any money."

My husband is very mild mannered. I could see he was very upset. He said, "What do you mean, we don't get any money?"

The loan officer explained that on a construction loan, like we had secured, you had to go out and purchase the materials, install them and then they would come out and inspect the work you had done. If that met with their approval, they would pay you.

We looked at each other in a daze. *Now what?* Could we find a plan B and be able to finish our project.

We left with all our paper work in hand, no money and knew we had to find a way to make this work. We got home and looked at each other and said, "Now what do we do?"

We finally decided to use our business credit line and buy the materials and then install them like the bank had explained we had to do. When we got the money after the banks inspection, we would pay our credit line back. We had a plan and we started in again working on our home to get it finished. It was really becoming a beautiful home. We had done so much planning and worked so hard for it. We would soon be finished, and have something worthwhile for all our efforts.

38

REBELLION RAISES ITS UGLY HEAD AGAIN

Things were really different with only one child at home. Only, my baby had changed into a teenager. Boy, that was a bad change. This sweet, lovable child suddenly became rebellious, and always wanted to be different with wild hair, wild clothes, and even a ring in her nose, and anything else she felt she could do to upset us. Her and Frank were always so close and then she suddenly turned on him, too, and broke his heart.

He had always loved her so much and could not understand what he had done to deserve this mean treatment. I tried to explain that even sometimes girls are that way with their own fathers. It was just a stage she was going through. But it did not help much. His heart was broken with the way she treated him and I tried to get through to her about her attitude and anger, but it didn't help.

Then, it started, "I am going to live with my dad. It will be better there."

She was running with a wild crowd, and the more I tried to reach her the harder it got. She was going to do whatever she wanted. She was very headstrong and nothing seemed to work. She always looked old for her age, and always ran with older kids. I was even having a hard time keeping her in school. That was not a priority with her. With her learning problems, it was hard for her and she had gotten tired of trying and tired of feeling stupid in school.

She was drinking and running and I was trying so hard to keep some control, but her friends and her partying were her life. Friends are very influential in there lives and no matter what you do, they have the most influence over them. I was up night after night waiting for her to come home and praying for her, and hoping I could do something to change this crash course her life was on. She looked so much older and was always let in the bars without even being asked for ID

So when she decided to find her father and get in touch with him about coming to live with him, I was almost relieved to get her away from her friends. I thought, *Well, maybe this will help to get her out of the crowd, and maybe she will listen to him.*

She had not had any contact with him for quite awhile, which didn't help her self-esteem. Kids always feel they are not lovable and take the burden on themselves when they do not get love from the parent that leaves. They don't realize it is the adult with the problem. I had tried to explain this to her many times, but it didn't help, she still needed some time with her father. Teenagers have so many feelings all bottled up inside, and I think children from divorces have many more things to cope with and feelings they don't understand about what has happened to their loving parents who were both once there. I don't know if they even understand their own feelings and are able to sort them out and figure out just who they are upset with.

She finally got in touch with her father and convinced him that she needed to come stay with him for awhile. Of course she was excited, the grass is always greener on the other side. By this time, he had remarried and had another child by this marriage. The woman he had married had an older boy about Cindy's age, so things had really changed. After months of running wild and threats and her terrible attitude, it was a relief to have her go and get a rest from it all. I also knew it was something I had to let happen and something she had to do. It was hard, but I knew the way to keep something forever is to give it away.

So off she went to a little farming town where he lived, out on a horse ranch, which I figured would be a good place for her to get her out of the city. I was not sure of the atmosphere she was going into because I had never met his new wife, and did not know for sure what their lives were like. I didn't have a choice at that moment.

She arrived, but after a few weeks I could tell that she really didn't fit in to that community. She was still trying to do her own thing and they had rules there too, which she did not want to abide by, either. So she stayed until Christmas when she came home for a visit.

After talking to him, I found out she had caused a lot of trouble there for him and his new family and he did not want to have any part of having her back again. He called her during Christmas and told her she could not come back. That was a terrible blow to her. She pleaded and pleaded, but he still said, "No."

She was really mad and confused now, and having to start all over again in another school in the middle of the school year would really be hard for her. Under much duress, I finally had to start her in school, but she was so behind and getting acquainted all over again was very hard.

One day she said, "I am not going to school anymore." She would not stay there and I was always getting calls that she wasn't there. So we went and talked to the school counselor to find out if we had any other options open to us so she could get her education. The counselor suggested that she go to a local college and get her GED, so we decided to do this and she was so relieved that she was finally going to get rid of this awful thing that had plagued her life for so long called school.

I was glad we decided to go this route because I knew there was no keeping her in school and she was going to be expelled if she missed any more classes. She finally finished this course and decided to go to beauty school, which was good training for her because she had always enjoyed working with hair. I knew she had to succeed at something for once in her life. She was so frustrated.

39

ANOTHER CHALLENGE

Well, we were completing our home and could see the end in sight. I had begun selling real estate again, it seemed easier because I had learned my way around and had learned to read maps, and adjusted to city life. One day when I was on the real estate tour, we entered this home. It was just framed up and needed someone to complete it. It was a beautiful home with a view out of every window of the lake, mountains, and the Seattle skyline.

I walked into this home and took one look and could see all kinds of possibilities. I turned to my associates who were viewing homes with me and said "I am buying this home." They all looked at me stunned as if I was crazy or something.

One said, "What do you want to buy this home for? You don't even have the other one finished yet."

But that didn't slow me down. I always knew what I wanted and this was something I knew would be a good investment for us. I knew we could do very well on making some good equity after finishing it and then eventually selling it.

So as we were driving away, I was writing up a sales agreement, determined to purchase this house. I finished writing up the agreement and called my husband who was working a ways away and said, "You better come look at this house I bought. I made the offer contingent on your approval and I want to get it finalized right away."

There was a pause on the other end. Then he said. "Is this another rental?"

He was used to me picking up deals when they came along. I said, "No...," trying to avoid the ultimate question, and then it came.

He said, "Do we have to move to this house?" I was afraid he was going to ask that question. I knew how much he loved the other house we had worked on for two years. It had been like his baby and he had done a lot of extra woodworking and special things to our home. We were just beginning to see an end to that project.

So I gulped and said, "Yes..." Silence.

He said, "OK, I will be there soon and meet you there."

I headed up there and soon I could see him coming. I was so anxious to show him my new find. Being in real estate, I could see what an opportunity it would be for us. I knew we had spent two years of every evening and every weekend working on finishing the other house, but if we wanted to get ahead, I knew we had to do it again.

When he walked in he had to agree with me, no matter how hard it was, he knew it was a good opportunity for us. He agreed and we finalized our agreement and presented it for review to the sellers.

All I had to do was get financing. I said I would never do that again. Never say never...you will eat your words, but here we go again. Only this time, my banker that I had worked with for quite awhile before we moved to the city had moved to the city too, and was working at a local bank. We had put lots of deals together in the past and I knew I could work with him, and be creative. I would have to with two houses to pay for.

So off to the bank I went knowing it would be a fight, but I was ready to go through with it.

Well the financing was finally completed. We knew we had to get busy and finish the other home we were in so we could start on the new one. After a few weeks, we were finished, but we decided we would finish the new one before we moved in because it was such a struggle and was so hard on your furniture with the construction dust and inconvenience of living there with a mess.

So the fun began. We began moving studded walls and arranging our new home the way we wanted it. It was an exciting adventure, and a great challenge.

After a year, it was finally finished. We put the other home on the market and got ready to move to the new home, near the lake. The market was good, so it didn't take too long to sell, but making two house payments was very stressful for one year, but we made it. Now we were on our way.

We moved into the new home. I noticed that my husband was really having a hard time. He was actually having withdrawals from selling the other home. It had became such a big part of him and he had done so many beautiful things with lots of special trim. I thought for awhile we were going to have to buy it back and that he would not be able to adjust to getting rid of it, but it got easier with time and we began enjoying our new home.

187

40

A MIRACLE

Cindy was back with her old friends and she had found some more that were even more dangerous. I was very worried about her, but her will was strong and she was drinking and running around. I never knew where she was or when she would be home. She finished beauty school, but could not pass her test because of her learning problem, dyslexia. Tests were always so hard for her, and she tried and tried without any success. She was becoming more and more frustrated, which didn't help things. Her attitude towards Frank was so bad, I wished that I could do something to change everything that was going on, but nothing worked.

One night as we were sleeping, there was a telephone call. It was the police. She had been in a bad accident, smashing her car into a rock wall on her way home from the bar. I got dressed and ran to the police station. There she was, bleeding from her face, legs and arms, with her front tooth half missing. She looked terrible, as if she had been in a battle and lost. I guess she had. They had suspected that she was drinking so they took her to the police station. I don't know why they did not call an ambulance, but anyway she was hysterical.

I signed her out and took her to the local hospital to be checked over. The car's door handle had gone into her leg, so she had a terrible gash there and she looked so bad I was afraid she had a concussion. Finally, they checked her over and she was only bruised and cut, and I took her home.

I knew, through my prayers, she had a guardian angel riding with her and my prayers had been answered. She was spared from death, especially after I saw the wall she hit and the way her car was damaged. She lay on the couch for quite a few days in a lot of pain. I thought this accident would wake her up and make her realize that drinking and running were not the answer for her life. I was sure God had spared her that night for a reason.

She lost her license because she refused to take a breathalyzer test and they suspected alcohol was the cause of her accident, but this did not slow her down. She continued to run with her friends and continued her wild lifestyle as soon as she could get going again.

After a few weeks, she healed up and got her teeth fixed, but her back was hurt and she continued to be under doctor's care for quite awhile. Living on pain pills really worried me, but she could not live free of pain.

Things went downhill from there and she was involved in many things that I don't want to go into at this time, but she was in for a life of despair and I couldn't help her.

I think this is one of the hardest things for a parent to see, your child's life going down and you not being able to do anything but pray. Keep praying for God's promises are true.

41

LIFE CONTINUES

Well we had several weddings.

My oldest son married a girl with three little boys, so he is getting his just reward by seeing how it is to be a stepparent, realizing what we went through.

Our oldest daughter has two children, and Frank's daughter has one child and we are still working through things we couldn't work through before. That is a blessing.

We have seven lovely grandchildren and finally our lives are our own. What a change, but none of this has been trouble free. We count our blessings everyday. We are enjoying each other and throughout our marriage we have continued to develop our relationship and our hobbies. Being sure that we always take the time to be interested in each other's hobbies and growing together. We were not strangers to each other when our children were finally gone. That is so important.

Don't put your whole life into your family and your job, because one day you will be facing each other, just the two of you, and you need to be friends and companions so you can enjoy your golden years together.

We have had many serious talks with the kids and are still working through our difficult times, and trying to figure out why things went the way they did and asking each other's forgiveness if there is any hurt we have put on each other. Healing is still taking place every time we get together. We are finding a new respect and love for each other, which wasn't possible when they were young and didn't understand marriage and parenting, and realize that parents make mistakes too. We don't mean to, but it happens. We are only human. Sometimes we are not proud of the way we handled a situation, or how the situation turned out, but we did the best we could under the circumstances.

So many times the kids would say, "This place is like a prison." But after they got out on their own, that prison looked pretty good at times. I guess they all go through stages when times are hard for them, too, especially the teenage years. We have seen many rewards, but I want to share a couple special things that have happened since the children have grown up.

One day when my husband and my oldest son were together sharing, Frank said to him, "Son you have become a wonderful young man and father."

He looked so special at Frank and said "If it wasn't for you Pa, that wouldn't have happened, and I love you."

I know he finally learned to love and trust and find love only through the love of this wonderful man.

There was another special time I want to share with

you. Cindy finally grew up and matured and Frank and Cindy have found a wonderful relationship. In fact, a few years, ago she was visiting us and he put his arms around her and she put her arms around him and he said, "Cindy, the battle is over and I am so excited because, guess what? We won..."

This was one of the most wonderful times in my life, as they hugged each other and found love once again.

42

HELPS FOR A GOOD MARRIAGE

1. Always make God the head of your family and marriage, and always be first in each other life. Allow your husband to be head of the household.

2. Always be sure you take time each day when you both come home to have a special time together, just the two of you without interruptions, and talk.

3. Make dates with your mate and stick to them. Mark off your dates on your calendar so you won't schedule something else that night. This makes each person feel important to the other one. The world always wants to tear that apart and take over your schedules.

4. Take turns planning your dates so each person gets to do something they enjoy and don't complain about what the other one schedules. It could be important to them, maybe not as interesting to you, but be interested.

You will be surprised how much you learn and enjoy just spending time together.

5. You don't have to spend a lot of money on these dates. Some of our best dates were just walking and talking, maybe sharing a hamburger. Keep it simple so you don't strain your finances which takes some of the spark out of your date.

6. Spend time away from the children. No matter how old they are, you need time together without interruptions.

7. Pay bills together so you both know what you have to spend, and don't let one person be the scapegoat for paying bills.

8. Try never to both be angry at the same time. Stand back, count to thirty and look at the situation before you say something you will be sorry for.

9. Never yell at each other unless the house is on fire. That hurts feelings and is hard to repair.

10. If you must criticize, do it lovingly. Try to put it in a way that he or she will be helping you if they do it another way.

11. Never bring up mistakes of the past. They are in the past, keep them there. You can't change them no matter how many times you bring them up. Bite your tongue if you have to.

12. Neglect the whole world rather than each other.

13. Never go to sleep with an argument unsettled. It will be harder tomorrow and besides you won't get a good night's sleep, and making up is so fun.

14. At least once every day say a kind or complimentary word to your life partner. It will also help you realize what you appreciate about them. They need to feel special in this cruel world and if you aren't making them feel special, someone else will.

15. When you have done something wrong, admit it and ask for forgiveness.

16. At least once a year make a list of the things about your spouse you fell in love with. Don't dwell on the things that he or she does wrong.

17. Remember, being a father and provider is not an easy job. Love him for the way he tries to do this job and remember he is only human and is going to make mistakes, just like you.

18. Pray together. The Bible says in Matthew 18:19, *"I say unto you, that if two of you on earth agree about anything you ask for, it will be done for you by my Father in heaven. For where two or three come together in my name, there am I with them."* Remember there is power in your prayers for your marriage and for your family.

19. We did an interesting survey in one of our women's groups at church. The young women were complaining about their husbands never doing anything around the house without being nagged, which is bad for a marriage. One older lady came up with some advice for the younger ladies which I thought was great and they agreed to try it. You make a list for your husband of things you want done, go over it together and place it on the wall where he can see it. Tell him you are not going to nag about these things and you know he will take care of them. Then, after you post the list, each time you go by the list stop and pray for your husband and pray for him to take care of these duties. We had lots of smiles when the reports came in from these young women how this worked in their marriages, and all the nagging and fights it saved in their marriages.

20. Remember to tell each other you love them, everyday. Remember guys, women need at least eight hugs a day to feel loved. Remember they are different than you.

21. Wives, don't ever point your finger at your spouse when having a discussion or put your hand on your hips when taking to your spouse. This triggers bad feeling and they feel they have to defend themselves.

22. Take time at least once a week to do something special for your mate.

23. Men, love your wives as Christ loved the church.

24. And men...don't forget to put the toilet seat down. This is of the utmost importance.

43

Helps for Putting Families Together

1. Never disagree in front of the children. When a child asks permission to do something, yours will always come to you and his will always go to him. Never decide without consulting your mate. The children will try and put pressure for a fast decision on you, but always go to a secluded place with your mate and decide if you will come up with a yes or a no. Come back in agreement and be united, no matter how much crying and/or opposition to your decision. Never let them know who was for it and who was against it, then you are never the wicked step-parent on decision making. Women see things different than men, especially when it comes to daughters. They learn at an early age to manipulate their fathers.

2. Don't make plans without consulting your partner and talking it over. Make sure the children do not dictate your life and what you do. You can be there for them, but

you can't be friends with your children and be an authority in their lives. If you are doing what's best for them, most of the time they will not be happy about it, but that's OK.

3. Keep your home a haven for everyone involved to come to, not a battlefield. Try hard to keep it that way, even if you have to ask someone to leave.

4. One day a week, have sharing among the family to air problems and any other differences. Try and draw each one out.

5. Never let the children come between you, no matter what. Remember, they will be gone soon and will have their own lives. Don't let them ruin your marriage.

6. Have meals together whenever possible. It brings a feeling of security to your family and helps unite you. I know this is hard at times, but make a real effort.

7. Stick to your principles and if a child or children won't abide by the rules, serve them an ultimatum to conform or be punished. Take action. Always carry through with the punishment you have decided together.

8. Remember, in cases where children need to go live with the other parent, the best way to keep something forever is to give it away. You may have to let this child go to the other parent's house to live for awhile. Don't be blackmailed by your children.

9. Make your children share in the household responsibilities, no matter how young they are. Always make them share in major purchases they want for themselves. They will take better care of it and it will have more value to them. They will learn responsibility for their actions.

10. Don't get discouraged about being the wicked stepparent. Speak up and tell your spouse how you feel about things. It is better to get them out in the open and deal with them. If you don't, you will take it out on the child in the end through your resentment for them.

11 Find another couple that you can exchange baby-sitting with, so you can both take turns having an evening alone together without the expense of hiring a baby-sitter.

12. Pray for your children everyday before they leave, to help them face this world.

13. Always give the kids duties. Don't try and do it all by yourself. No matter how young they are, this will help them learn and feel like they are part of the household. Maybe at first they won't do it like you want, but praise them for what they did and they will do it better the next time.

14. Let the children know that when one of you speaks or tells them to do something, the other spouse will back you up on your orders.

15. Control your home and what the children watch on TV and hear on the radio. Don't put up with loud music. It is your home. Remember, you are the adult, they are the children.

16. Assure the children you are not trying to take the other parents place, but they are to obey you and your rules in your home, and respect you and your opinion while there.

17. Always tell your child you love them. Explain from time to time that you can love a spouse and a child, too; that you have enough love to go around for both.

Teach your children how to fish and work at being independent, so they won't be in need. Remember, as your children get older (at least 20 and away from home) you will get smarter every day. Hang on to this through those teenage years.

May God bless both you and your marriage.

To order additional copies of

Yours, Mine and We Decided Not to Have Ours

please send $15.00
plus $4.95 shipping and handling to:

Cecelia Garceau
Box 2785
Sequim, WA 98382

*Quantity Discounts are Available